# CHANGE FOR THE POOR

A Guide to Restoring Lives *with* Those in Material and
Relational Poverty

Mark F. McKnelly

**Renown Publishing**
**www.renownpublishing.com**

**Change for the Poor / Mark F. McKnelly**
ISBN-13: 978-1-952602-59-7

The changes and transformations I have seen through some of the men in the Restoration Program are nothing short of incredible. Some of these men have bounced back from a lifetime of challenges and adversities. It's unbelievable to watch the improvement as these individuals advance through the phases of the Restoration Program as they are restoring their lives.

**Sean Ziverk | Probation and Parole Officer**

The heart of the Restoration Program at Victory Mission is to be more than a treatment program. The Restoration Program is totally committed to the complete work of Christ in the hearts and lives of men and women, and the total restoration of the people that God created them to be.

**Mark McDonald | Credentialed Counselor: MS, CRADC, CGDC, CRPR, MARS**

I know of no other program in Southwest Missouri, or in all of Missouri and surrounding states, for that matter, that helps restore men and women to health—spiritual, mental, emotional and relational—like that of Victory Mission's (VM) Restoration Program. As the Director of the Good Dads program, which Victory Mission incorporates into its programming for all the dads in their Restoration Program, I've seen story after story of hope and healing over the past three years. As a clinical psychologist who provides supervision for the mental health providers serving at VM, I am continually awed and blessed by the changes I've seen in the lives of their residents. Some otherwise "hopeless" cases have a new life and hope for the future because of their experience. We are all better for the work that Victory Mission does at no charge for the benefit of the men they serve. Our community is safer and more productive with people like them.

**Jennifer L. Baker | PsyD MFT | Founder and Executive Director of Good Dads, Inc**

It is awesome to see how God is using Chaplain Mark and the Restoration Program to introduce people to Christ and His amazing grace. I have witnessed broken and hopeless men who have nowhere else to go transformed into hope dealers and Kingdom builders through the Restoration Program. This is what being the hands and feet of Jesus should look like!

**David Stoeker | National Recovery Advocate | Author of *Hope Dealer* | Credentialed Counselor: LCSW, CPS**

This book will challenge most of your assumptions on how to help "those" people. Get ready to listen and walk with those coming out of family chaos and poverty. Mark blends grace, compassion, truth, and story together to bring us a how to book in the process of change and life transformation.

**Jason Hynson | Executive Director of Victory Mission + Ministry**

*Change for the Poor* is an incredible resource when it comes to planning and implementing a restoration program. There is no reason to recreate the wheel now, thanks to Mark and this book. An easy-to-follow guide, practical applications, and informative truths about serving the poor make this book a must-read for anyone planning to start or reform a restorative process.

**Jody Dow | Executive Director of The Springfield Dream Center**

I have worked with Mark for over five years now. The program he created is solid, and it is a program we support and recommend in our community. The principles are Biblical and effective, [and we see] proof through changed lives.

**John Stroup | Executive Director of Freeway Ministries**

I met Mark when he started working in outreach and recovery ministry at the church. It is his personal experience every day in the trenches that has rocketed his understanding of how to transform lives. The end product of changed lives through the restoration program is truly amazing, and its graduates have been legitimately restored!

**Alon Fisch | Executive Director of New Beginning Sanctuary | Member of Missouri chapter of National Association of Recovery Residences housing task force | Board Member of Missouri Coalition of Recovery Support Providers | Founding Partner of Springfield Recovery Community Center**

Uncomfortable balance, that is what Mark McKnelly brings in Change for the Poor. This wholistic approach to chronic poverty is highlighted in Chapter Four, where he discusses three relational approaches to helping the poor. Paternal: doing "to" others. Maternal: doing "for" others. Transformational: doing "with" others. Another uncomfortable balance is struck by the third principle of restoration: accountability for those being restored. Want real results? Then apply these principles.

**Jack Smart (US Missionary with the Assemblies of God, CEO of Rural Freedom, Director of Living Free at James River Church)**

At The Well Church we have seen and experienced first-hand the incredible life change that has come through the Restoration program and curriculum led and created by Mark McKnelly, through Victory Mission. Mark knows and understands that true restoration only comes through a personal relationship with Jesus Christ, and he is committed to this truth. In Mark's book, Change for the Poor, he allows us into this truth and process as he teaches us the three principles of restoration, which are relationship, structure, and accountability. I am excited to use this book as a resource in our Redemption Ministry at The Well and share it with others who are answering the call of the Gospel of Jesus Christ to go and make disciples.

**Selena Freeman (Lead Pastor of The Well Church)**

I want to thank everyone who worked with me while on the ministry staff at Schweitzer Church in Springfield, Missouri, for eight-plus years. The restoration work I am involved in today is a movement of God in large part because of those years with you amazing men and women of God. Then, of course, huge thanks to Victory Mission + Ministry. My amazing leaders here, David Myers, Jason Hynson, and the Board of Directors, have allowed me to come in and implement the vision for what is now the Restoration Program. This work also would not have been possible without our entire staff, the volunteers, and the restoration men and women themselves. Without all of them, this would be no more than ideas and theories. My prayer is that this book will equip those serving in any type of restorative ministry context and lead to the certifying and planting of future Restoration Programs.

I also want to thank those who made this book possible financially: my earthly father Kenneth McKnelly, Alon Fisch and David Stoeker with the Springfield Recovery Community Center, philanthropist and friend Steven Warlick, long-time prayer partner Joshua Wood, and the gracious men in my life group from James River Church.

# CONTENTS

# How to Read This Book

This book is an introduction and guide to a very practical process that can transform the way individuals, churches, and organizations work with those in extreme material and relational poverty. There are three ways you can approach *Change for the Poor*.

## Learning Individually

If you read this book on your own and receive some insight on how to better reach out to, and truly help, people in extreme poverty, then I would consider it a success. If you work or volunteer in a poverty alleviation context and you apply the principles where you are, with your "sauce" as they say, I would also consider that a success.

## Learning Collectively

Using the discussion and reflection questions in a group setting makes for a four-session small group experience that any church or organization could use to become better equipped to do restorative ministry with those in extreme poverty.

**Launching Restoration**

If after reading this, you, your church, or your organization should become interested in learning more about the restorative principles and processes found in this book, please visit www.changeforthepoor.org. I would love to connect with you and discover how I might be helpful in coaching or collaborating with you, wherever or however you are serving those in extreme poverty.

# Introduction

Have you ever worked with someone in extreme poverty? I am talking about more than rolling your window down and giving money to the homeless man on a street corner, or serving food in a soup kitchen, or writing a check to a non-profit. What I am asking is this: have you engaged a poor person in a conversation, listened to their story, and attempted to meet their needs in some way? Did you feel uncomfortable or uncertain in that experience? Maybe you had high hopes for what your help could accomplish in alleviating their pain, even transforming their lives. How did it go? In over a decade of vocational ministry, the number of conversations I have had with well-meaning people who have reached out to someone in extreme poverty are innumerable, and in most cases, the intentions were good but the results were not.

*Change for the Poor* is for the person who wants to better serve those in extreme material and/or relational poverty. You may already be serving the poor, as a job or with volunteer time; if so, that is great. I hope this book can better equip you to do that, inspiring you to keep going in that very difficult endeavor. You may not have spent much time at all in serving those you would consider poor. That is great, too. In *Change for the Poor*, I will introduce an effective method to reach the poor that will transform their lives and yours. While I believe this book can benefit anyone seeking to improve the effectiveness of their work with the poor, the principles are guided by Christian faith and practice.

As I finish writing this book, I will have been a follower of Jesus for thirteen years. Upon my coming to faith in Christ, the Lord opened my eyes to those around me and, by the Holy Spirit, motivated me to help those in extreme poverty. How many of us would not want shelter if we were homeless, a meal if we were hungry, clothes if we were naked, visits if we were in prison or the hospital, and so on? I concede that a stumbling block for many Christians is that they simply do not want to take the time and effort to truly know and journey with someone in extreme poverty. That stumbling block is tragic, but it's something *Change for the Poor* does not address. However, since you picked up this book, I am going to assume that your heart is captivated by the possibility of being part of bringing someone out of total destitution and desperation to a place of hope and restoration.

If that describes you, and yet you find yourself today on the sidelines of engaging people in extreme poverty, I assume you struggle with one or both of the most common reasons for inaction that I have seen and personally experienced. First, many do not know where to start or whom to serve. Second, many others have helped those in extreme poverty before, have had bad experiences, and have since retreated. This book's approach offers a way to break free from both of those reasons for inaction. Be encouraged. You can do this.

The word used throughout this book to describe the kind of approach I believe can bring change for the poor is *restoration*. To ensure we're on the same page, for the sake of simplicity, let's contrast restoration with relief. *A relief approach is effective to meet immediate and external needs and is often appropriate when needs arise in a person's life because of situational reasons.* Some examples of situational reasons for relief include natural disaster, unexpected death or hospitalization, serious accident or injury, house fire, divorce, and job loss (if losing jobs is not a pattern). I want to acknowledge that the relief approach does impact lives and helps people. I endorse the relief approach when those being helped are experiencing poverty as a result of situational reasons. And further, some people are gifted and called to help others using the relief approach. I have seen that to be true, I respect those who serve in the relief field, and I do not intend for this book to devalue the relief approach when rightly applied.

It is important to remember, though, that needs also arise from cyclical reasons, also referred to as chronic or generational reasons. When the needs of those we are serving come from cyclical reasons, the right approach is restoration. A short-term season of relief will likely be a part of the initial stage of serving someone in extreme poverty, regardless of the reason, but for long-term change to take place in a person's life, the approach must transition from relief to restoration. *The restoration approach is marked by the investment of a significant amount of financial and relational resources over a long period of time.* It is the only approach that holds the key to bringing wholistic change to a person living in extreme poverty (see Chapter Eight to discover why I spell wholistic this way). Restoration is my passion. *Change for the Poor* will describe in some detail how to take a restorative approach toward serving the poor in your individual life, small group, church, or organization.

I in no way intend to repeat all of the great work that has been done by so many who have written books addressing poverty alleviation. Books like *Toxic Charity*[1] and *When*

*Helping Hurts*[2] were foundational for my growth in effectively working with those in extreme poverty. I recommend reading those in addition to this book before diving into or reforming your work with the poor. I wrote this book because I believe it adds a unique perspective and process to a healthy and growing conversation on how we can better bring lasting change for the poor.

I am not an academic, and I am still learning from mistakes and continually collaborating with others who do the same work I do. I would stop short of calling myself an expert. My heart is one of a *practitioner*. I have worked with those in extreme poverty daily for nearly a decade now, first as a pastor in a church and now as a chaplain in a non-profit organization. In the trenches of restorative ministries, I have come across principles that have worked to restore the lives of people who find themselves in extreme material and relational poverty. At Victory Mission + Ministry, I am currently the lead chaplain of the *Restoration Program*, where I work with men and women reentering society from incarceration and recovering from addiction. In fact, I am in thirteen years of recovery from an addiction that made a train wreck of my own life and have found the same principles to be crucial in my restoration. This book is born from a burning desire to share what I have seen God do through the restoration principles we are practicing with others.

Without further delay, there are three restoration principles I believe are necessary to bring about change for the poor: relationship, structure, and accountability. I will share scriptures, illustrations, stories, and explanations to back up why I am so confident that when these principles are present, restoration has an exponentially higher likelihood of taking place in the life of a person in extreme poverty.

I do not see many three-legged stools these days, but when I grew up in the '70s and '80s, we had three-legged stools in our kitchens. While the three-legged stool illustration may be a bit outdated, it is effective for what is being presented here, in terms of how important each of the principles is to restoring lives. Relationship, structure, and accountability represent the three legs of the stool. If any of those three restoration principles is missing or lacking in strength and integrity, then the stool does not hold up and the fullness of restoration that God desires for a person simply will not be realized or sustained.

Okay, let's put to bed a possible objection you may have about the use of the word restoration. The *Merriam-Webster* definition of *restoration* is: "a bringing back to a former position or condition."[3] At some point you might think, if people are products of chronic or generational poverty, having spent their entire lives in utter hopelessness and destitution, then what part of their lives are we attempting to restore them to? That is a good and fair question. Theologically speaking, Christianity teaches that all humans are image-bearers of God (see Genesis 1:27). One of God's desired results of salvation is that all Christians would be restored into the image of Christ (see Romans 8:29). And after God begins His saving work in a person, He continues doing a work that will eventually bring them back to their originally designed state of being (see Philippians 1:6)—a state of restoration.

Thank you for taking the time to read this book. A word of warning to anyone who has yet to experience the restoration approach to change for the poor: it will fundamentally change you to the core. The highs will be high, and the lows will be low. Restoration, working daily with those in extreme poverty, is not at all glamorous. As a pastor friend of mine rightly puts it, "this ministry will rip your heart out." In 2020, our ministry walked through the tragedy of experiencing seven overdose deaths of men who were at one time involved in our program. In some of those cases, we had to make gut-wrenching phone calls to their loved ones, while grieving with those they left behind in the program. Restoration ministry is not for the faint of heart; at the same time, it is also soul-satisfying. There is no vacation destination, sensual pleasure, or accomplishment that compares to it. Every life radically and forever changed through your faithfully walking someone into restoration is worth all the time and effort you will pour out. I am both excited and prayerful for you.

# First Principle of Restoration: Relationships

# Motivated by Compassion

*And Jesus went throughout all the cities and villages, teaching in their synagogues and proclaiming the gospel of the kingdom and healing every disease and every affliction. When he saw the crowds, he had compassion for them, because they were harassed and helpless, like sheep without a shepherd. Then he said to his disciples, "The harvest is plentiful, but the laborers are few; therefore pray earnestly to the Lord of the harvest to send out laborers into his harvest."*

**—Matthew 9:35–38**

A church that I was serving in 2013 was touching thousands of people through a tremendous number of outreach ministries. However, it began to weigh heavy on our hearts that few, if any, of those being served were making their way into the church, breaking the cycle of poverty, and becoming followers of Jesus. Several initiatives were put in place to address this. One that I was fortunate to lead was a Sunday-night meal and outreach worship service called Church @ the Center. It was tasked with building a bridge into the life of the church from its outreach ministries, to break the devastating cycles that lead to material and relational poverty.

There were so many lessons we learned the hard way during that process. It was significant because it was during this season of ministry that God did a deep work in my heart about why I would commit to spending a lifetime serving those in extreme poverty. And one key way He did that was through the above scripture (Matthew 9:35–38). I took our leadership team back to those verses repeatedly from 2013 to 2017. To this day, as I pour myself into the lives of hurting people, the Holy Spirit still uses that passage to give me a much-needed heart check. There is much to learn from that great passage, but two words have always captivated me when it comes to how I relate internally with those I serve: *compassion* and *prayer*. Those two words create a strong conviction in my heart that it is impossible to be in a loving relationship with those I serve without having compassion and praying for them. Let's look at the first word, compassion, which speaks to what motivated Jesus, as found in verse 36.

**Compassion.** How did Jesus relate to all of those crowds that gathered around Him? Matthew records in his Gospel that Jesus had compassion on them. He did not become judgmental. He did not become cynical. He did not grow weary of them. His heart did not harden toward those He saw as confused and helpless people. He had compassion on them. There is a real thing in caring ministry known as compassion fatigue. I have experienced it first-hand, and it can sneak up on you. You begin to depersonalize those you are serving. You put them into categories with others who suffer from the same consequences of poor life choices, areas of underdevelopment, disabilities, or (pick your sub-category). You may say things like, "Well, what did they think was going to happen?" or "When will they figure out that doesn't work?" or "I am not sure what they thought we could do for them." When those kinds of attitudes begin to take hold, I know I am moving further from the kind of compassion for the hurting and helpless that Jesus had. No one would argue that a lack of compassion is a good starting point for launching into relationships with hurting and hopeless people.

Instead, Jesus was continually fueled by the compassion He had in His heart for people whom He saw as sheep without a shepherd, lost and helpless. If or when you lose compassion for the broken people you serve, please take a step back and search your heart. If God's love for you cannot rekindle a flame of compassion for the people He is bringing to you for a restored life, then I would respectfully ask you to find something else to do with your time.

I realize I promised a primarily practical guide to restoring lives, and you might be wondering at this point what your motivation for serving has to do with that. I believe that being honest about what truly motivates us has a very practical impact on the lives of those we serve. This book is unapologetically Christ-centered, so I have no choice but to urge you to ask yourself what motivates you to help the poor. Is it really love for your neighbor? There is a practical and detailed description of what God considers to be love in the New Testament: "Love is patient and kind; love does not envy or boast; it is not arrogant or rude. It does not insist on its own way; it is not irritable or resentful; it does not rejoice at wrongdoing, but rejoices with the truth. Love bears all things, believes all things, hopes all things, endures all things" (1 Corinthians 13:4–7).

15

Certainly, that paints a perfect picture of the loving compassion of Jesus Christ. I must admit that it is not always descriptive of my heart while serving—not all the time, and not for everyone. Is it descriptive of how you love those you serve? In our context of poverty alleviation, the verse before the above passage says this: "If I give away all I have, and if I deliver up my body to be burned, but have not love, I gain nothing" (1 Corinthians 13:3). *The Bible teaches that we can serve to the point of giving our stuff and ourselves away and yet, it remains meaningless if we do not have love.* Please take a moment to let that sink in.

You must regularly ask yourself compassion questions, and ask those around you to hold you accountable. This would have a profound impact on all of your relationships, and the relationships you have with those you serve are certainly no less important. Are you serving because you truly have loving compassion for people who cannot help themselves out of the metaphorical pit they find themselves in? Or, be honest, is it because it makes you feel good about yourself to help people? Or does it make you feel less guilty about all the material possessions and financial wealth that you have? Or do you do it because people praise you for how much good you're doing in the world? Or is it because you have deep, unhealed hurts in your own heart or destructive habits in your own life, so you use serving others to make up for, or take the focus off, of these personal struggles? Real heart questions, I know. Stop reading and ask them now. If you can't honestly conclude that your motivation is from an overflow of the love of Jesus in your heart and life, expressing itself in compassion for hurting and hopeless people (see Galatians 5:6), then I again suggest that you find something else to do with your time. That might sound harsh, but people can and do get hurt when we serve them out of selfish or misguided motives.

On a recent morning entering a Walmart Neighborhood Market, I began a short conversation with a homeless man outside. While I was asking him questions and trying to help point him in the right direction for the help he needed, a woman walked up with her wallet already out of her purse. Effectively interrupting our conversation, she gave the man a ten- or twenty-dollar bill and then told him she was so sorry for where he found himself. Following her into the store, I found the courage to kindly share with her that I worked with the homeless and that giving them cash is not always the most helpful approach. She unleashed a venomous attack on me for "robbing her of the blessing she receives in giving money to the poor." I thought it best in that public setting to just bow out of that moment and move on, but her motives were very much exposed in that response, were they not? Her giving was as much or more about her being blessed than about her truly blessing the homeless man.

You see, when your motivation to serve others is more about serving a need you have in your heart, then the person you serve is more of a project to be completed than a person to be cared for. Certainly, they need you at some level for relief or restorative ministry, or they would not be at the metaphorical doorstep of your life, church, or organization. They have needs that are likely very outward and obvious, and the relationship dynamic of their need for you in the beginning stages, at least, is unavoidable. But as a Christ-centered caregiver, serving from the wellspring of the loving compassion of Jesus, you should not need those you serve. If the answer to any of the motivation questions like the ones above was yes, then you serve from selfish motives. *A self-serving need to serve will limit your ability to love and serve people selflessly.* In romantic relationships, the clinical term for this is codependency; the biblical term is idolatry.

The Licensed Professional Counselor (LPC) on staff at Victory Mission + Ministry that sees and serves the men, and sometimes the women, in our Restoration Program so often reminds the chaplain team to avoid this kind of unhealthy motivation. He reminds us that we must love the men in a deeply personal, compassionate, even covenantal way, but that we must divorce ourselves from the outcome. In other words, we cannot attach ourselves too much to the good or bad choices they make. We cannot find ultimate purpose and joy from those we serve experiencing amazing life transformation, and we cannot become overly devastated if those we serve manipulate us, fall short, or walk away from us.

Going through the process of regularly checking your heart is remaining true to a favorite proverb of mine: "Keep your heart with all vigilance, for from it flow the springs of life" (Proverbs 4:23). The first way to recognize if you have built the foundation for a loving relationship for those you serve is to find out whether or not you have compassion for them. The second way can be found in the final two verses of the passage in Matthew chapter 9.

## Chapter One Notes

# Empowered by Prayer

*Then he said to his disciples, "The harvest is plentiful, but the laborers are few; therefore pray earnestly to the Lord of the harvest to send out laborers into his harvest."*
**—Matthew 9:37–38**

The second word that continues to captivate me is found in verse 38. Matthew described the traveling ministry of Jesus and how He drew crowds of people to Him who wanted to know more about the kingdom that He was proclaiming and demonstrating. In closing the recap of Jesus' ministry, Matthew recorded Jesus telling the disciples to do one thing in response to the harvest being ripe and the workers being few. In this passage, there is only one command given: *to pray*. I am truly blown away by that. Are you? I believe that in this command, Jesus has given us profound perspective and guidance on what to do in response to having compassion for the crowds of lost, confused, and broken-hearted people we encounter in this world. It has been nearly seven years since that first stood out and inspired me, and only last year did I truly start to pray as Jesus instructed us to. *Father, forgive us for not praying as if it were the primary force behind any Kingdom ministry in Your name!* I pray as I write this that it doesn't take you as long as it did me to grow weary of using natural resources to fight a supernatural battle. All of our relationships change when they are saturated in prayer.

I believe lack of prayer to be the primary explanation for the lack of fruit in the ministries that I have led for years. Not praying for those we serve is disobedience to the one command given in Matthew 9:35–38. Is the harvest great? I think so. Are the workers few? I definitely think so. So, what do we do about that? Jesus told us, about as straightforwardly as He could have. Pray! Will God, by His grace, still change some lives without the kind of prayer Jesus instructed us to pray in this passage? Sure He will, because He is that good. But I can tell you this much: when I decided to take the peer leadership team, known as Residential Supervisors, in the Restoration Program and call us down on our knees every day—to plead with God to send us more workers and to move in power—things went to another level in the ministry.

So why do we not pray as Jesus commanded us to? I mean praying like it is the most important thing we can do to bring about change in the lives of hurting and hopeless people. I have asked small- to medium-sized groups of Christians over the years why they think we do not pray often or fervently enough. The most common reason I have heard is a lack of time, due to our schedules being so busy.

The great sixteenth-century reformer Martin Luther is often quoted as saying this about his daily prayers in light of his daily workload: "I have so much to do that I shall spend the first three hours in prayer."[4] So please join me in losing the lame excuse that we do not have time to pray. The busier your day is, all the more reason you have to pray! Can we admit that we make time for the things in our lives that we value? Can we begin to believe that God will move mountains not only to redeem but also to replenish the time we spend in being faithful to His word?

Allow me to share a couple of reasons why, I think, we do not spend the first three hours of every busy day in prayer; both observations come from the same Matthew 9:35–38 passage. First, we forget how much more we resemble the sheep than Jesus—possibly less often and less dramatically than those in extreme poverty, but still, we are sheep. And like sheep, we need to be led—in all areas of life, to be sure, but definitely in prayer. *Without a shepherd, sheep wander off into dangerous places, and prayerlessness is about as dangerous of a place any Christian can find themselves.* That is most certainly true for a Christian working in the oftentimes dark trenches of restoring people's lives.

The second is that we lack a sense of desperation to pray for what we truly do want to see happen in the lives of those we serve. The word translated simply as "pray" in most English versions is translated "beseech" in the New American Standard Bible[5] and "pray earnestly" in the English Standard Version.[6] The Message paraphrases verses 37 and 38 this way: "'What a huge harvest!' he said to his disciples. 'How few workers! On your knees and pray for harvest hands!'"[7] You get a sense that Jesus was trying to convey just how desperate we need to be for fervent prayer.

The sad truth is that we just do not operate in a daily

mindset or perspective that prayer is so crucial. If we did, we would "pray earnestly to the Lord" as Jesus asked us to. I would urge you to invest time and effort in finding good leaders who can help you learn how to pray like this, and to invest time and effort as well in being transformed by a renewing of your mind (see Romans 12:1) when it comes to praying for the hurting people you are serving. Then, be prepared to see the relationships with those you are serving dramatically change when you pray earnestly for them. I hope I have made the point that prayerless service to the poor will prove to be far less effective.

There is another serious aspect to prayerlessness we find in the prophet Samuel's farewell speech to the people of Israel. The prophet said this is the way he felt about praying for the people he served: "Moreover, as for me, far be it from me that I should sin against the LORD by ceasing to pray for you, and I will instruct you in the good and the right way" (1 Samuel 12:23). It should be a sobering thought for any Christian leader or caregiver that failing to pray for those God has called us to serve is disobedience. This means not praying for those I serve not only hinders their chance for restorative life change, but it is also a sin against my Lord. I don't know about you, but I am compelled now more than ever to pray as Jesus commanded us to in Matthew 9:35–38.

The implications for not being empowered by prayer should be apparent to us by now. A. W. Tozer, a leading twentieth-century American pastor and author, went as far as to propose that "if the Holy Spirit was withdrawn from the church today, 95 percent of what we do would go on and no one would know the difference." I believe what Tozer was saying was that we can develop enough manmade methods and models for doing ministry that we become desensitized to the power of God to change lives. Whether or not that was true decades ago or is true today, why don't we apply the cause and effect to ourselves and our ministries? *If the Holy Spirit were removed from the ministry you lead or serve in, how much of it would go on without anyone noticing a difference?* There have been far too many months, sadly years, of my life as a Christian leader in which the answer to that would have been: a lot of ministry would continue without much noticeable difference.

I don't know about you, but I am worn out with trying to help internal change happen in human hearts through external methods. I am ready to view prayer as if it is the primary and power-providing way God is going to change the eternal destinations and internal heart conditions of those I serve. As Oswald Chambers said, "prayer does not fit us for the greater work; prayer is the greater work."[8]

I love listening to great communicators when they preach and teach. And I love learning today's top leadership concepts and strategies. I do. I am not condemning any of that outright. Give some time to that kind of thing. Yet I have learned the hard way that all of that type of learning is insufficient to give you or your organization the power it needs to become a movement of God. I am talking about a movement of God's Spirit that begins to transform lives from the inside out at such a depth that everyone stands back in awe of God's work.

That is truly what is happening right now in the Restoration Program. Dozens of men's lives are being changed so radically that no funding source, program structure, or leadership team can take credit for it. As I write this, we have recently launched a women's Restoration Program so that we can provide the same life change for women in our community. I cannot reiterate enough that what I just described measurably increased when the peer leaders in the program and I hit the floor in humble prayer, desperate for God to bring us workers, save the lost, heal the brokenhearted, and restore lives.

I want to add that we are not the only ones who fervently pray for Victory Mission. I am confident many are pleading with God and believing that prayer is our primary weapon in the battle to restore lives. I can only give specific voice to how it happens in the ministry I personally lead. And might I suggest something that will help make prayer a part of your restoration culture? Schedule it. Put it on your calendar. Daily, if possible. I tell the men in the Restoration Program, when they share any change they want to make in their life, "Get a plan. Get a partner."

Prayer meetings are not naturally occurring events in the normal environments of American life, especially work life. So, choose a place everyone can gather, at a specific time during the day, and then follow through on it. *Treat your scheduled prayer meeting like it is the most important meeting of the day, because it is.* Start by reading some Scripture, and then briefly share some timely praises and petitions. A Psalm, Philippians 4:6–7, or Matthew 9:35–38 would be a good choice to launch into group prayer like this. Then change your posture. If you are able and feeling brave, hit your knees. If not, I recommend that you hold your hands up or hold them open to God. Our physical position can impact our spiritual posture during prayer. Each person can then briefly share. Our prayer meetings of three to ten people range from five to twenty minutes in length. There truly is a feeling after most of these times in prayer that we have done the most important work of restorative ministry.

I would suggest that the selfish and/or misguided motivations we talked about in the previous chapter deepen and continue due to prayerlessness. Something happens in our hearts when we make praying for the people we serve a priority—something supernatural. We begin to have the compassion that Jesus had for hurting people when we pray for the people we serve. When you do that, you find a cycle you will never want to break, one that builds a foundation for deeply loving relationships motivated by compassion and empowered by prayer.

In the next few chapters, we will continue by diving into our first principle of restoration: relationships. For the sake of the content so far, I suggest that you take a break and process it all through the first set of reflection and discussion questions. If you are reading this individually, find a notebook or journal to go through them. If you are doing this with a group in your church or organization, you can also meet up in person or online to discuss the questions with as much openness and honesty as possible. You will be amazed at how the relationships with those you serve become more fruitful when those relationships are enriched by the time you spend together praying and learning how to restore lives and bring *change for the poor.*

## Chapter Two Notes

_____

_____

_____

_____

_____

_____

_____

_____

_____

_____

_____

_____

_____

_____

_____

_____

# Introduction, Chapter One, and Chapter Two Questions

1. Where are you right now in helping those in extreme material and relational poverty, individually and/or organizationally? Be brutally honest.

_____

_____

_____

_____

_____

_____

_____

_____

_____

_____

_____

2. Describe, in your own words, the difference between a relief and a restorative approach to helping the poor. Give some examples of each.

_____

_____

_____

_____

_____

_____

_____

_____

_____

_____

_____

3. Read Matthew 9:35–36 again. From this passage's recap of the traveling ministry of Jesus, what stands out to you?

_____

_____

_____

_____

_____

_____

_____

_____

_____

_____

4. Think about times when your motivation was not compassion for those you were serving. What was that like for you, and/or them?

_____

_____

_____

_____

_____

_____

_____

_____

_____

_____

_____

5. Read Matthew 9:37–38 again. What are the implications of Jesus telling us to pray as a result of the harvest being ripe and the workers being few?

_____

_____

_____

_____

_____

_____

_____

_____

_____

_____

_____

_____

6. Consider your calendar. How much time do you spend learning from leaders, teachers, academics, experts, and practitioners versus how much time you spend praying for God's provision in your restorative ministry?

_____

_____

_____

_____

_____

_____

_____

_____

_____

_____

_____

7. Oswald Chambers said, "Prayer does not fit us for the greater work; prayer is the greater work." What would have to change for that to describe your perspective on, and practical application of, prayer?

_____

_____

_____

_____

_____

_____

_____

_____

_____

_____

_____

# Return on Investment

*A new commandment I give to you, that you love one another: just as I have loved you, you also are to love one another. By this all people will know that you are my disciples, if you have love for one another.*

**—John 13:34–35**

In the business world, there is something known as return on investment, or ROI for short. When financial resources are put toward anything, a good investor will naturally want to see a return. Jesus was also aware of and employed this principle. His method for making disciples was to invest deeply in a small number of men and women over three years and to expect that investment to provide a return. In this case, the return was taking His message of the good news of the kingdom of God to the ends of the earth. Implied in the above passage is Jesus' profound love for His followers—and that they would then invest the same kind of love in their followers, and on and on it would go. Fast forwarding to today, consider the context in which you are serving: investing in them the way Jesus invested in people should be a high priority. Now imagine investing relatively little time with someone you are serving and ask yourself if they would feel as much love from you as you intend.

Sadly, the widespread method of ministry to those in extreme poverty in America today has become more transactional than relational. I'll be honest: transactional was my method at first. I remember after coming to Christ in 2008, for years, I just wanted to "help" anyone I could. The love of Jesus had flooded into my heart, so I started giving money to the homeless man or family on the street corner, chasing down folks who came in our church's food pantry to try to help them get a bike or clothes for an interview, or assistance for late electric bills and rent, etc. What I experienced at that time was something that many Christians have experienced: frustration, exhaustion, and heartbreak. Men, women, and families were assisted in getting an *immediate* need met, but the *underlying cycle* that produced their need remained. *Once a short season of relief is given, for help to become restorative, a two-way relationship must be formed.*

I would say that from my observation, churches, nonprofits, and government agencies in America today have become enamored with programs. I am not entirely against programs. You might be thinking, don't I chaplain a program? Yes, I do. However, I hope this first principle of restoration will safeguard us from thinking it is about any restorative program. It is always about loving relationships, within any given program, working to restore people's lives. It is shocking to me that when God came on His rescue mission in the person of Jesus Christ, He did not write books, build buildings, create programs, or start institutions. If you know your Bible, you know that's true.

What was the method Jesus used to transform lives and the world? He spent three years with a small number of devoted followers, teaching and preparing them to follow in His footsteps after His crucifixion, resurrection, and ascension back to His Father in heaven. That approach goes directly against the grain of how faith-based or secular organizations and government agencies have engaged the poor for a very long time. The relationship Jesus had with people was not complicated; he simply spent time with them and loved them while doing everyday life kinds of things; weddings, funerals, festivals, dinners, recreation, and so on.

At the deepest level of your heart, if you want to help people break generational cycles of poverty, addiction, and criminal thinking, *you must be engaged in an ongoing, open, and honest relationship with those you are serving.* That means, whether you are operating in a more structured program or more of an individual process, either setting is only there to facilitate the relationships of those you serve. The people are not there to make the program go, or to allow it to have statistics that prove it is necessary and vital; the program is there to serve the principles of restoration: relationship, structure, and accountability. We will unpack these principles later in the book. Consider how many churches and organizations are not seeing the return from their investments of time and money because the focus is on numbers in crowds and budgets. The return I refer to is restored lives.

One lie I believed for a long time was that to make a large impact in any serving ministry, I had to have contact with a large number of people. The kingdom of God is often called an upside-down kingdom. An example of that upside-down truth, lived out in the life and ministry leadership of Jesus Himself, is this: *the deeper you go with the few, the greater the potential impact you will have on the many*. In exhausting our resources at a surface level for many people, we may feel like we are getting a lot done, but I have experienced that and seen others do the same, oftentimes resulting in one of two things: First, the one serving burns out because we were not created to go a mile wide and an inch deep in our relationships. Second, the ones being served will have immediate and external needs met, yet will have underlying issues that go unaddressed because of the lack of depth in the relationship.

*Spending hours per week with a very small group of people will at first feel like a misuse of your time.* It did for me, and it will for you. We have been hardwired by a production-based, go-go-go, do-do-do, numbers-reporting culture. You will need to buy into this being an upside-down paradoxical truth or else the relationship leg will collapse and your restoration stool will fall flat. There is a sign on one of the dorm room doors in the men's Restoration Program that captures what the twelve to eighteen months of their restorative process is ultimately designed to accomplish: *Cycle Breaker*. I love that! The time we spend over that year or longer, sometimes hour by hour, is breaking a cycle that will impact relationships in this generation and for generations to come. I do not believe that happens at a dramatic level outside of significant relational time.

Look back on your childhood. Who were the people who had the greatest positive impact on your life? I would venture to say it was the ones who spent time investing in you as a person, in developing your character, values, and priorities. For most it was a parent or family member, but often I hear that it was a beloved teacher, coach, youth pastor, foster parent, or mentor. Our program has a Licensed Professional Counselor (LPC) on staff, so I highly value having clinical resources at our disposal in ministering to people in material and relational poverty; but no doubt, our society is moving more and more toward an exclusively clinical approach to helping hurting people. The "housing first" model for ending homelessness and the "medication first" model for treating addiction, for example, are becoming the standard in virtually all sectors of poverty alleviation, even some faith-based ones. I am not saying there is not anything to learn from those models; what I am saying is that if you intend to wholistically restore the lives of those in extreme poverty, then I believe there is no substitute for spending frequent, meaningful, and intentional relational time with those you are serving. Our mission statement at Victory Mission + Ministry is that "we share God's love through intentional relationships for the restoration of a broken-hearted world," because our vision statement is that "every life has purpose."

I recently reflected on those I have invested the most time in over the years. One became a pastor, is planting a network of house churches, and has published his first book; two others have gone into full-time pastoral ministry. Another worked in part-time vocational ministry while raising her little ones; yet another has his local minister's license and has started Bible college classes. And another is leading one of the outreach ministries he at one time utilized for assistance, while three restoration graduates are currently apprenticing to possibly become restorative leaders themselves someday. I am awed and amazed at how many lives God is impacting through that relatively small number of people I have closely led

I wonder how many more lives my leadership could be impacting today if I had spent more focused and intentional time on fewer people in my early years of ministry. One of the things most of the men who have come into the Restoration Program will often say, even early in the process, is that they feel loved just as they are. They feel relationally accepted simply because they are in our program and made in the image of God. *When a high priority is put on intentional relationships, there is the highest possibility that those you serve will feel the love of God through you.*

In no way would I say that the principle of restoration is easy; without question, the relationship principle of restoration is very messy. It is a terribly difficult and inconvenient endeavor to enter into a relationship with a person whose life has completely fallen apart, who sits before you completely without hope. That said, the principle itself is not complicated. In my opinion, it is not restorative ministry until an authentic two-way relationship has formed and significant time is invested in each person being served.

# Chapter Three Notes

_____

_____

_____

_____

_____

_____

_____

_____

_____

_____

_____

_____

_____

_____

_____

# To, For, or With

*And Jesus came and said to them, "All authority in heaven and on earth has been given to me. Go therefore and make disciples of all nations, baptizing them in the name of the Father and of the Son and of the Holy Spirit, teaching them to observe all that I have commanded you. And behold, I am with you always, to the end of the age."*
**—Matthew 28:18–20**

Again we have the words of Jesus Himself, this time after His resurrection and immediately before His ascension back to heaven. It is commonly referred to as the Great Commission. About ten years ago, I was traveling in South Florida and came across my favorite church mission statement so far, by a long shot (if you weren't aware, all churches have mission statements these days). It was at Calvary Chapel Fort Lauderdale. Their mission statement consists of two words from verse 19 of Matthew 28: "Make disciples." That's it!

However, that still begs the question of how we make disciples. The passage itself points to at least three things: baptizing, teaching, and abiding. We are not going to jump ahead to our structure and accountability principles yet, but bear with me in the context of our restoration principle of relationship. I will grant you, the first one, baptism, is a brief, albeit crucial, episode in the process of making disciples, but the other two are highly relational.

The second part is teaching. Considering the teaching aspect of making disciples, I will ask you to do some critical thinking. Jesus said we are to be teaching those who follow us to obey everything He commanded. Is that even possible without spending significant time *with* those you are teaching? Forget for a moment that the Bible records that three years of daily, relational contact with a relatively small number of people was the approach Jesus took to teach those who heard this Great Commission. Think logically about how much relational time it will take with those we serve to transfer what we know and have learned to them.

You may have noticed in the book's subtitle that I put the word *with* in italics. This guide is a guide to restoring lives *with* the materially and relationally poor. The *with* is very intentional. I was at a conference years ago, before I made the shift to relational ministry, where a woman who had planted a church in an impoverished urban neighborhood of a large U.S. city spoke. Her name was Kathy Escobar. This reference is not an endorsement of her theology or overall approach to ministry, which I admit I am neither fully aware of or informed on, but I share the story because I remember to this day how greatly affected I was by her contrast of three different relational approaches to helping people: *to* them, *for* them, or with them. The *to* approach I would summarize as being paternal, or as I mentioned earlier, transactional. A check being written or serving at a one-day outreach event—

that kind of thing. The *for* approach I would summarize as being maternal, or doing for someone what they cannot do for themselves. Moving furniture for a disabled person or watching kids for a single mom. That kind of thing.

Before outlining the *with* approach, I will again concede that there are times and places in which the *to* and *for* approaches can be healthy and necessary. Natural disasters no doubt require *to* and even, to some extent, *for* approaches. A *to* approach in such a time could include financial support of a church or non-profit relief organization. A *for* approach in such a time could include joining a short-term mission trip to help reconstruction efforts. A *for* approach could also be personally providing temporary childcare for a single mom while she is working, or helping a disabled widow without a support system. My point in the context of this chapter and book is that as Christians, we must recognize that for restorative ministry to begin taking place, we cannot be satisfied with helping those who are in extreme material and relational poverty until we are in relationship *with* them.

*I would describe a* with *approach as highly relational and personal, marked by prayer, heart-level truth-in-love conversations, and wholistic support.* In the Restoration Program, we put categories to the idea of speaking into the whole life of a person: they are spiritual, relational, personal, vocational, and financial. We'll unpack those later, but in the context of a *with* approach, it is important to point out that no area of life can remain unaddressed. In your relationship with God, are there any areas of your heart and life that He allows you to keep from Him?

I will never forget when the *with* approach to ministry became real for me, through leading that Sunday-night meal and outreach service. The classic transactional model of ministry was exhausting our leadership team because we were filling all of the main serving roles. When we would serve the 80 to 120 in attendance, it was far too few people doing ministry *to*, and it was *for* far too many people. After attending that conference and being impacted by the idea of a *with* approach, we started recruiting our regular attendees, especially those who had signed up for the discipleship program we offered, to join the serve teams and begin giving back. It was a game-changer.

If someone in a sober living home had a clean driving record but no car, they could drive the church van to pick people up for the service. If someone could get there one hour early, then that meant they could help prepare and serve the meal or put out the donations on our community "treasure table." If someone could sing a little or play an instrument, then we'd talk to them about being on the worship team. More than half of the prayer and tech teams, and virtually all of the hospitality and setup/breakdown teams, would end up being men and women who were used to coming to this kind of outreach service with their hand out.

Do you see what this does for the relationship dynamic of the haves versus the have-nots, or the givers versus the takers, or the caregivers versus the helpless? It shatters it. It does not discount or ignore the amount of restoration needed in the life of a person you are serving. What it does is uplift them in the relational dynamic and allow them to feel like you are *with* them in the process of restoring their lives. There is a method of developing those in extreme poverty called Asset-Based Community Development (or ABCD). ABCD combats the unhealthy dynamic explained above by engaging people with questions and conversations that focus on what they have, not what they lack, and then digging in to find out how those assets can be leveraged to break their cycle of poverty. There is a lot of good content online about ABCD, and I encourage you to check it out. I believe one of the beautiful things about ABCD is how it can naturally foster *with* relationships.

Another way I have seen *with* relationships greatly improve the restorative process in the ministries I have led is how they promote natural opportunities for teaching moments through simply doing regular everyday kinds of things together: preparing the community meal, stacking chairs, creating the worship slideshow, passing out flyers for the upcoming outreach event, etc. *Unfortunately, in our day, offices, classrooms, and coffee shops have become the common arenas for leading or helping people.* Again, I go back to the ministry of Jesus, where His office was around the campfire unpacking with His disciples what happened that day. His classrooms were the fields and roadways, on mountains and seashores. His coffee shops were deep water wells and wedding parties. When I began inviting the men and women I was leading to do ministry *with* me, teaching them became more natural and much more relational. It became a true *with* approach to doing relational ministry. It did not focus only on what they did not have yet, but on what they could bring to the table now.

Getting *with* relationships started in your ministry does not have to be difficult. Ask yourself and those you are serving these types of questions: What is it that I am doing, or have done, for someone that they could start doing for themselves? Simply empower them to take that over. What do the people I am serving love to do, and what are they good at? Take that list and explore the possibility of a new project or ministry being started through their passion, talent, or skill set. That is exactly how the "treasure table" ministry began at the Sunday-night outreach service.

Can the *with* approach get messy? Absolutely, *I promise it will get messy*. If you want a clean and mess-free ministry, then check out on the relationship principle and the entire restoration approach now. However, as messy as it is, it is so much fun watching a person join in the process of their restoration and begin to feel like a part of the ministry that is helping them.

# Chapter Four Notes

# Finding Your Burden

*He has told you, O man, what is good; and what does the
LORD require of you, but to do justice, and to love kindness,
and to walk humbly with your God?*

**—Micah 6:8**

The passage above has been referred to as the Great Requirement, and it paints such a beautiful picture for the context of serving *with* people. Do justly, treat people fairly, and advocate for their being treated fairly in this broken world. Love mercy, show kindness, and bring tangible blessings to people. Walk humbly with your God, and guard against making anything you do all about you. These biblical requirements provide great direction in the search for whatever specific people-group God will give you a passion for serving.

As mentioned, I have found my calling to be in relationship *with* men and women recovering from addiction and/or reentering society from incarceration. Does that mean you should commit your life of relational ministry to the same demographic? Absolutely not. I will say this, though: I believe the only way you will sustain long-term fruitful ministry to those in extreme poverty is if you have what is known as a "burden" for that people group. I also believe in my heart that every Spirit-filled Christian knows already, or can know through a process of prayer and discernment, whom they have a burden for. Do you know? Is it people trapped in generational poverty? Is it troubled youth? Is it the chronically unemployed? Is it people stuck in addiction? Is it people going through the revolving doors of jail and prison? *Do you need to go through a process of prayer and discernment about whom your burden is for?*

Remember, when searching for your burden demographic, that the restoration process is designed for men and women experiencing what I am calling extreme material and relational poverty. It could be that you find your heart breaks for a demographic who find themselves with a reasonable amount of resources and have some commitments they can keep—people who may have come to their current place of need primarily from situational rather than cyclical types of circumstances. If that is the case, then the intensity of something like a Restoration Program may not be necessary for them. Plus, that partially resourced person is also someone who likely will not feel the need to commit to a long-term restorative process. However, if you do find that your heart breaks for people who fit the description of being in extreme material and relational poverty, due to cyclical and chronic types of circumstances, then I assure you, something like a long-term Restoration Program is necessary, whether they believe it is or not.

I would like to help you look closely into how you can find

whom your burden is for. I hope you are excited, because I can testify to the fact that nothing will fill your heart quite like walking into the specific calling God has placed on your life! *If you do not yet know whom your burden is for, the first step to take is prayer.* Simply ask God to reveal it to you. This sounds like a Sunday school answer, I know, but don't breeze past it. Ask some spiritually mature people in your life to join in the supernatural step in this process. Prayer fits right in with Micah 6:8, the Great Requirement, because to pray genuinely, you have to walk humbly with your God.

A second step is to test out different serving opportunities and see how it goes. Sign up to serve at a local food pantry or homeless event. Join an addiction recovery meeting or group at a nearby church. Become a mentor or tutor to a young person through your neighborhood school or Boy's and Girl's Club type of organization. Find a jail or prison ministry and talk to the leadership, or even make a trip with them to one of their meetings. In communities of any size, the opportunities to get involved are more numerous than you might think. Do your research and then try something. Try *something*, even if it turns out not to be the people-group you end up being called to serve. Christians find it far too easy to hide behind the devout-sounding words, "Well, I am still in a season of prayer about that." The action does not necessarily undo the effectiveness of prayer in our lives; sometimes, God combines prayer and action to reveal His path for us.

A third step you can take is a personal assessment. The SHAPE Assessment was created by Pastor Rick Warren and Saddleback Church in California. SHAPE stands for Spiritual Gifts, Heart, Ability, Personality, and Experience. We use the SHAPE in the Restoration Program, and it has been helpful to walk our men and women through the process of discerning where God might be calling them to serve. The H section helps one discover for whom God has put a burden on their heart. One of the online resources for the SHAPE is www.freeshapetest.com, where you can take the assessment online. SHAPE is not the only assessment tool out there. Find one you like and fill it out. See what you learn about yourself and your burden.

Now I would like to inspire you with stories about some people who found whom their heart broke for and the result has been a dramatic amount of change for the poor.

Dr. Jennifer Baker is an amazing woman who found her burden. She is a psychologist who recognized through her practice that cycles of poverty, crime, and overall relational brokenness continued at an exponentially higher percentage in homes without an involved father than in ones with a father in the picture. As a result, Dr. Baker found her burden to be helping fathers to become actively engaged in their children's lives. She is now leading New Pathways for Good Dads, part of a state-wide program in Missouri to help at-risk dads be more connected with their children. Good Dads includes highly interactive parenting and relationship classes, but goes beyond the classroom by advocating for men on their child support and with letters for family court if they are making real efforts to be actively involved in their children's lives.

Pastor John Stroup was a felon and a self-described "knucklehead" before he gave his life to Christ. Once God changed his life and built his character, He confirmed John's burden for those trapped in lives of addiction and criminal activity. John planted a non-profit called Freeway Ministries that serves as an outreach to those he now has a life-long burden for. Freeway runs weekly worship services in partnership with local churches as an effort to build a bridge into the church for a people-group who avoid Sunday-morning church environments. Freeway also has discipleship houses where men and women from his burden demographic can pursue a relationship with God and often find sobriety, employment, family reunification, and more.

Scott Warren is retired with a background in business, and his burden is for those who are unemployed, underemployed, and even unemployable. He knows that soft skills and a biblical understanding of the purpose of work can make a huge difference in a person's vocational future. Scott is currently the director of Jobs for Life at Schweitzer Church. Jobs for Life (JfL) is a biblically-based workforce development program and curriculum that I have seen first-hand impact hundreds of people's lives. He has not only led over twenty sessions at Schweitzer but has also been instrumental in getting two other sites certified to offer JfL in Springfield, Missouri, and he coordinates with the twenty-plus JfL business partners in southwestern Missouri. In 2019, Scott's passion for and leadership in this ministry were recognized at JfL's annual conference. Because of his burden, now hundreds of men and women in one community have been equipped to get and keep jobs, and to glorify God through their work.

The above examples are relatively large in scale and influence. Please allow them to inspire but not intimidate you. If the work you do serving your burden demographic does not produce quite the same impact by the world's standards, it does not mean you are falling short of the calling God has on your life and ministry. Every single restored life matters to God.

# Chapter Five Notes

# First Principle: Relationships

1. Read the passage at the beginning of Chapter Three again (John 13:34–35). How does that change your understanding of being in relationship with those you serve?

_____

_____

_____

_____

_____

_____

_____

_____

_____

2. What do you take away from the fact that Jesus Christ did not write books or manuals, build buildings, create programs, or start institutions?

_____

_____

_____

_____

_____

_____

_____

_____

_____

_____

3. *The deeper that you go with the few, the greater the potential impact you will have on the many.* Do you believe that to be true?

_____

_____

_____

_____

_____

_____

_____

_____

_____

_____

_____

4. Looking back on your developmental years, who were the men and women who had the most positive impact on your life? Explain how and why.

_____

_____

_____

_____

_____

_____

_____

_____

_____

_____

5. Read the Great Commission passage again (Matthew 28:18–20). How should the instruction to teach those we serve what Jesus taught us affect our relationship with them?

_____

_____

_____

_____

_____

_____

_____

_____

_____

6. Share your thoughts on the church mission statement, "Make disciples." What is your church, organization, or

personal mission statement? Would it have to change to directly, or even indirectly, point you to intentional relationships?

_____

_____

_____

_____

_____

_____

_____

_____

_____

_____

7. How does the idea of having those you serve come alongside you more in your day-to-day work make you feel? Be honest: maybe nervous, scared, or excited? Or some other response?

_____

_____

_____

_____

_____

_____

_____

_____

_____

_____

_____

8. Whom do you have a burden for—what people-group? If you know, please share how and when you came to know whom your heart breaks for. If you do not know, share when and how you plan to discover your burden.

_____

_____

_____

_____

_____

_____

_____

_____

_____

_____

_____

9. Which of the stories in Chapter Five inspired you most? Why?

_____

_____

_____

_____

_____

_____

_____

_____

_____

# Second Principle of Restoration: Structure

# Trust the Process

*Trust in the LORD with all your heart, and do not lean on your own understanding. In all your ways acknowledge him, and he will make straight your paths. Be not wise in your own eyes; fear the LORD, and turn away from evil. It will be healing to your flesh and refreshment to your bones.*
**—Proverbs 3:5–8**

In 2019, a man in the Restoration Program got a letter for termination of parental rights from family services in a different state. He had been in our program about one year prior and left to move in with a woman. He admitted the relationship was one reason for leaving, but the other was that he was trying to find a permanent address to use to get his kids back. Unfortunately, the relationship went bad, other things in his life went worse, and he went back to prison. He came back to us upon release, and we gave him a re-entry, which we sometimes allow with a one-year suspension if they leave again. While he was back at the beginning of the program, he received the above-mentioned letter for termination of parental rights.

His mentor was a rock for him, as were our counselor, his home church, and many of his peers in the program. He knew this time that no matter how hopeless life looked, he must stay in the restorative process because he could trust the outcome to God. He now tells of a night in a worship service where he fully and finally handed his children off to God, praying that no matter what it cost, he would trust His process and promised to trust their lives to Him. God not only protected his children's safety over that year, but He also ended up blessing them all with full reunification.

We were excited to work with family services, along with a key partner program, New Pathway for Good Dads, and helped him get full custody of his kids. He graduated from the program, and we handed one of our Phase 3 houses off to him so that his kids could come to live with him full-time. His story illustrates the kinds of restorative blessings that often come to those who put their faith in God and trust that He will make a straight path out of their restorative process.

As I have mentioned, this is not a theologically driven book. However, it would provide an incomplete picture of what we do in the Restoration Program if you were left unaware of a core Christ-centered aspect of what we teach and practice: *we teach that if they believe God brought them to the Restoration Program, they can trust our restorative process.* We do not try to convince the men and women in our program that they can one-hundred-percent trust us as leaders, or even trust every rule, requirement, and restriction that is in place for them to follow. I will often say that I sleep well at night knowing that enough resources are being poured into each participant that if they will trust our process, they will walk away in twelve to eighteen months equipped to live a restored life.

One fruit, or benefit, of trusting the process for the Christian believer is that their effort can be a burdenless effort (see 1 John 5:3). If we are burdened by our effort, then we are not resting in the easy yoke of Jesus (see Matthew 11:28–30). I am not saying this is easy, but I am saying it is possible, when we put our trust in the promise from Proverbs 3, that God will make a straight path for us. Frankly, that is how God designed us and desires for all of His children to live. A common example I have seen in our program is men and women trusting God, and our process, so whole-heartedly that they walk around with a peace that truly surpasses understanding, even while facing pending or active charges, upcoming court dates, or the likelihood of spending time in prison (see Philippians 4:7). That reminds me of the mindset Paul had when writing a relatively short letter from a prison cell to the church in Philippi, where he mentioned the words "rejoice" and "joy" sixteen times. I have no hesitation in saying that if those you serve can truly trust your process, it will dramatically transform the way they pursue a restored life, and it will especially impact their ability to persevere when things get hard.

I believe that in many environments where those in extreme poverty are being served, the opposite mindset is present and likely even encouraged—a mindset that is always striving, always unsettled, at least to a degree. When thoughts of striving continually run in the background of a person's mind, it produces discontent and uncertainty that can quickly derail the restorative process. Producing or perpetuating a mindset with that kind of instability in a life that is already chaotic and stressful is in no way beneficial and can lead to increased hopelessness, even in the midst of what looks like a very healthy environment for them. I placed this chapter as the first on the restoration principle of structure because what people believe about themselves and their future greatly influences how they face requirements they're asked to complete, rules they're asked to follow, and restrictions they're asked to submit to.

One structured way we seek to embed the foundational "trust the process" mindset is through what we call the Soul Detox. The Soul Detox is our participants' first six weeks in the Restoration Program. This is the period of time with the most restrictions: no phone, electronic device, or unsupervised access to the internet or the outside world, and no leaving the official program area without at least one person who is off of their Soul Detox. The name Soul Detox was born out of the idea that just as our bodies need to detoxify from drugs and alcohol, our souls also must detoxify from the good, bad, and neutral things going on in the outside world that so easily distract us from the focus needed to restore our soul.

The Soul Detox is one built-in teaching tool for trusting the process, because for six relatively short weeks, what they have seen as necessary aspects of life on earth are taken off of their daily grid. When the participants' Soul Detox is over, they should always be able to look back to a time when all they had was shelter, food, clothing, and people who loved them—and see that it was more than enough. There are certainly other ways to lead those you are serving into trusting God and your restorative process. However, we have found that the lessons learned during the Soul Detox can help them see beyond all that distracts them from walking by faith and not by sight (see 2 Corinthians 5:7).

The Soul Detox is not only formational; it is a make-or-break season in the restorative process. We tell the men and women when they come in that if the Soul Detox works how it is designed to work, they will have:

- tuned in enough internally to identify their life-controlling issues.

- submitted to God and the leaders He brought into their life.

- learned to recognize and prioritize needs versus wants.

- developed the skill of active listening.

- started exercising spiritual disciplines and healthy rhythms of life.

- experienced waiting on God's timing.

If you are a faith-based person or organization, do not underestimate the importance of building a foundation for your participants to trust the restorative process that you have laid out for them. If you are not operating in a faith-based environment, then I would ask that you heed the warning from the earlier paragraph about creating an environment with continual striving and uncertainty in the mindset of your restoration participants. In either context, most people coming out of extreme poverty will find the idea of burdenless effort a completely new concept, so be prepared for it to hopefully draw them in but potentially push them away. A very real and all too common outcome is the sabotaging of their own restoration process out of fear of the unknown.

# Chapter Six Notes

# Time Is of the Essence

*Go to the ant, O sluggard; consider her ways, and be wise. Without having any chief, officer, or ruler, she prepares her bread in summer and gathers her food in harvest. How long will you lie there, O sluggard? When will you arise from your sleep? A little sleep, a little slumber, a little folding of the hands to rest, and poverty will come upon you like a robber, and want like an armed man.*

**—Proverbs 6:6–11**

We had a young man in his early twenties in the Restoration Program who we deeply loved and whose story would break your heart. Growing up, there was no parental or primary caregiving figure present in his life who loved him unconditionally. After a few months with us, and even with some breakthroughs in his spiritual life, we sadly had to remove him. He lacked the ability, or it could be argued, the willingness, to be on time to classes, devotions, volunteer assignments, and more.

When the alarm clock went off, he would sleep right through it. When we set an alarm across the room, he would get up, turn it off, and go back to sleep. When he would go out on Saturday or Sunday afternoon, he would miss that evening's program requirement because he lost track of time. We focused on this and worked specifically with him for weeks, increasing his counseling sessions and requiring the use of a daily planner, but nothing proved to help him with the simple life skill of making it somewhere on time. Be prepared—challenges like these are not uncommon when working with those in extreme poverty.

Like many, I love the practical wisdom in the Old Testament book of Proverbs. One of the many things you can take away from the above passage is that Solomon gives the ants high praise for their efficient use of time, for being diligent in their efforts. A clear implication in the seasonal aspect of the metaphor is the fact that God gave the ants the time necessary to store up the provisions they would need later. *It is especially true that time is of the essence in terms of how we work to restore the lives of those in extreme poverty.* God has given us all an ample supply of the resource of time. And a very common learned behavior and roadblock for those in extreme poverty is the misuse of time and a lack of understanding of its importance as a resource in their lives.

In some cases, you will find laziness, like was described in both the young man and the above proverb, to be so severe that the person is simply not ready to engage in a wholistic restorative process. We will touch on what to do in such a case in our third principle of restoration: accountability. However, if the person is showing themselves to be a willing restoration participant, you will find that time management is something requiring serious attention.

Misuse of time for those in extreme poverty is due to at

least the following two factors. The first is a lack of purpose; they just have not had a compelling reason to be diligent or intentional about life. Other aspects of the restorative process will address that—intentional relationships and some of the classes mentioned in an upcoming chapter. The second is the lack of basic life skills and habits. I have found that men and women with a long history of unemployment or underemployment, homelessness, addiction, and/or coming from generational poverty simply do not have what employers call "soft skills," and an important one of those is the life skill of time management.

I usually cringe with some hesitation when I speak, and now write, about this topic because of how this part of the restoration process can seem condescending. These are grown ups we are working with, right? Yes, they certainly are adults, literally speaking, and in some ways, they are advanced in terms of both skills and abilities (you have heard the term "street smart," I am sure). *However, most coming out of extreme poverty have lived in such unstructured and undisciplined environments for so long that there is a great need for developing as close to a 24/7-structured schedule as staffing, security and/or peer supervisory systems allow.*

I will never forget the day I was sharing my heart with the men in the program in early 2018 about how successful people don't waste time or take naps, how no one needs more than eight hours of sleep per day, and so on—I think you can guess the kind of life skills speech I was barking at them. One of our shyest men very meekly raised his hand, and when I called on him, he said this: "Chaplain, we hear what you are saying, but we don't even know how to live." That was a pivotal moment for me. The revelation I received was that one of the things people coming out of extreme poverty desperately need is structure—a "sun-up until after sundown" kind of structure. No guesswork. For example, below is the Phase 1 (first three months) weekday schedule in the Restoration Program:

- 6:00–7:00 = Breakfast
- 7:00–7:30 = Morning Group Devotion
- 8:00–12:00 = Volunteer Assignment
- 12:00–12:30 = Lunch
- 1:00–2:00 = Class #1
- 2:15–3:15 = Class #2
- 3:30–4:30 = Chaplain Check-in
- 5:00–6:00 = Dinner
- 6:00–8:00 = Evening Class or Free Time (classes for a minimum of four nights/week in Phase 1)
- 8:00–8:30 = Evening Group Devotion
- 9:00–10:00 = Chores
- 10:00 = Curfew
- 10:30 = Lights Out

The only large blocks of free time come on Saturdays, but other than that, the structured environment and responsible routine are developing a real-life skill. Going back to the passage in Proverbs, we see that laziness will lead to poverty and scarcity. It should go without saying that poor time management will be a significant roadblock in your work to bring change for the poor.

In 2010, Laura Vanderkam released a book titled *168 Hours: You Have More Time Than You Think*[9], 168 being the number of hours we all have in our week. In the book, she refutes the commonly used phrase, "There just aren't enough hours in the day." Through the study of census data and intense personal interviewing, she concluded that we not only have enough time in the day but that we have no idea where our time is going. *It turns out that most people report the use of their time with high amounts of inaccuracy.* So why share this in a book addressing change for the poor?

Because, I would venture to say, if the premise of that book is correct, then we ourselves as caregivers are most likely not good time-managers and have believed the lie that there is just too much to do and too little time to do it in. Looking at our restorative process through this lens, I now understand why, when I share with people all that we require of men and women, especially in Phase 1, they look at me with such amazement. "Wow, that is a lot! They do all of that for twelve straight weeks in Phase 1?" The answer is, I've watched hundreds do it and you would be surprised how much downtime they still have. Lesson? If you are on the fence about adding a class or an hour of volunteering or another session of counseling to their week, probably add it. They, and frankly you, when structured and organized, have more time than you think!

In the Restoration Program, we ask for a twelve- to eighteen-month commitment, and we structure the program requirements carefully to follow that timeline. *Consider the investment of time it will take to restore the life of someone who has experienced chaos, trauma, abuse, neglect, violence, addiction, and/or crime for years, perhaps their entire life.* For them to show up at the doorstep of your life, church, or organization, there is no doubt significant relational brokenness and material destitution accompanying them. Think about the challenge of restoring a person from a background like that in just a fraction of the time it took them to become, as people like to say, "broke, busted, and disgusted," or "sick and tired of being sick and tired." I hope that learning this truth about time impresses on you the importance of every day and hour for the people in your restorative process.

To share just how short the time is that our men and women will invest in the Restoration Program, we roll out some percentages for them. Taking the minimum amount of time required for completion, one year, I calculated how much one year was in comparison to the rest of their lives. Here is what I came up with. It shocked me to see how low these numbers actually were:

- If they live 60 more years, 1 year is only 1.7% of the rest of their life.

- If they live 50 more years, 1 year is only 2.0% of the rest of their life.

- If they live 40 more years, 1 year is only 2.5% of the rest of their life.

- And if they only live 30 more years, 1 year is still just 3.3% of the rest of their life.

The perspective benefit for us as caregivers is to drive

home just how short a period of time we have to facilitate life-long change for those we serve. The perspective benefit for those entering a restorative process is to emphasize for them just how short an amount of time they are investing to experience wholistic restoration for the rest of their lives on earth.

# Chapter Seven Notes

# Five Areas of Wholistic Change

*The thief comes only to steal and kill and destroy. I came that they may have life and have it abundantly.*
**—John 10:10**

One of our full-program graduates, out of thirty-one, has fallen off of living a restored life. Three have relapsed, that I am aware of, but those three landed quickly on their feet and applied the restorative principles they learned while in the program. Admittedly, we don't monitor and cannot know how every area of the other thirty's lives are going. We do stay in enough contact with them to know that some have their struggles, certainly, but that overall their lives are radically transformed compared to before. The story of that one graduate's dramatic fall is tragic, and it has to do in large part with his leaving one area of life unrestored.

Even while experiencing tremendous breakthroughs and restoration in so many areas of his life, he remained in a highly toxic romantic relationship. Our beloved fallen graduate experienced healing over some devastating losses in his life, had a job with great pay and benefits, was plugged into a church, was taking care of legal obligations from past mistakes, and had enough money to buy some things he had always wanted. It seemed he was living a restored life, but his relationship with his girlfriend was so unhealthy that it brought his entire life back to where it was before the program. An ugly breakup, drug use, job loss, property damage, injury, and shame pulled him away from his church family and his friends from the program.

This heartbreaking story goes to show how just one unrestored area of someone's life—in this case, romantic relationships—can leave the door open for Satan to steal the rest of the work that has been done. Thank God we have learned from instances like these and now work to protect our men and women in each of the five vulnerable areas of life. For this reason, we have what we call a *wholistic* approach to restoring lives. If you are questioning why it isn't *holistic*— the more commonly spelled version of the word—there is a reason. Both are accepted and carry essentially the same meaning in our day. *Holistic* is indeed considered to be more appropriate in an academic context, but I feel the *w* in *wholistic* communicates a lot.

*A wholistic approach adopts the philosophy that all parts of a thing are interconnected.* In medicine, wholistic treatment is the treatment of a person as a whole—mind, body, and social factors. Do you see the connection to John 10:10 and Jesus having come so that we might have life, and have it to the full? When restoration has taken place, something or someone has been taken back to the originally intended design and purpose. A whole new creation. A whole new heart. A whole new life, and not just in one or a few areas of life.

The five areas of wholistic restoration for us are: spiritual, relational, personal, vocational, and financial. The story of our fallen graduate at the beginning of this chapter is an example of how crucial it is that we do not leave even one of the five wholistic areas untouched and, God forbid, unrestored. In another case, a person might be climbing out of poverty, spiritually thriving, repairing family relationships, planning to transition to a stable residence, satisfying their probation and parole, staying clean, and more. But if they cannot manage their money, then the stress of being evicted, broke, hungry, and homeless will likely jeopardize all they have worked so hard to restore.

Therefore, in the Restoration Program, we continue to see the importance of increasing how much accountability we require in observing that budgets are adhered to, savings balances are verified, and major purchases are approved. Furthermore, I will describe in depth the five wholistic areas of restoration, as well as outline a small number of the specific benchmarks we set within each of those areas to benefit those we serve.

**SPIRITUAL.** The Restoration Program is unapologetically Christ-centered. We respect faith-based programs that require a certain number of church services or Bible studies to be attended. We acknowledge that this is definitely helpful and even increases the potential for long-term recovery and restoration. In the way of structured requirements, we expect our men and women to do far more in their spiritual life than attend church services, classes, and groups. In addition to other spiritual requirements to be listed shortly, most importantly, we ask them to belong to, become members of, and remain deeply involved in what we call their home church. Specifically, by Phase 2, we require them to be giving financially, serving regularly, worshiping weekly, and meeting in person with an approved mentor from their home church.

The term *home church* is very intentional. *We believe the local church is God's means for making disciples of Jesus Christ.* Jesus told Peter that he was the rock on which He would build His church and the gates of hell would not overcome it (see Matthew 16:18). When the Holy Spirit came on the day of Pentecost, after Jesus ascended to heaven, the result was the birth of the church (see Acts 2:1–4). When the Apostle Paul traveled, he planted local churches by preaching and teaching the gospel, training and appointing leaders, and writing letters directly back to them about how to live in the context of a New Testament local church.

If you are a non-profit like us, we encourage you to partner with local churches. If you are an individual Christ-follower working to restore the life of someone in extreme poverty using the principles put forward in this book, we encourage you to partner with local churches. In both cases, the transitional strategy of phases we will look at later is designed for you to have a high level of influence early on with those in the restorative process, and then to slowly and intentionally help them commit to a home church for long-term discipleship. If you are a church seeking to launch or reform a restorative ministry, you can be both the restorative program and the home church, which has its advantages and disadvantages. Remember, I started a restorative ministry while on staff at a local church, and there are challenges. If you would like more information on those dynamics, I invite you to contact me directly. In the spiritual area of restoring lives, the home church is a vital piece, but there are more pieces to the spiritual puzzle. Some of the benchmarks in this area include:

- **Group devotions.** These morning and evening thirty-minute devotions help develop a daily rhythm and discipline. They also provide many opportunities for volunteers to come in to serve and lead the men and women.

- **Soulwork.** The word *homework* carries with it some baggage, so we use the word *soulwork* instead. We want them to see soulwork as a tool more than a rule. Soulwork consists of a weekly report, mentor and church attendance reports, and Scripture & prayer tools.

- **Scripture and prayer.** As part of their soulwork, we ask that they document times in Scripture and prayer using Bible reading and prayer method tools we provide. Those tools are perfect for the Study Hour class times and for those who may need to be given additional or disciplinary assignments.

- **Memory verses**. Every week, we collectively memorize a verse or short passage of Scripture. Participants share how successfully they memorized it and, more importantly, in a chaplain check-in, what they learned from slowly processing it.

- **Mentoring.** In Phase 1, they see a Phase 3 participant, and by Phase 2, they have a mentor from their home church. Weekly mentoring is part of the

CHANGE FOR THE POOR

structure principle of restoration but is obviously key
to the relationship principle as well.

- **Classes**. *Walking by Faith* is the core spiritual curriculum that teaches what was introduced in the previous chapter.

- **Testimonies**. Before they transition through the phases, we want to see, in writing, evidence of healing, how they are being spiritually restored in the way they understand and have experienced forgiveness, and an account of what has changed since they entered the program.

**RELATIONAL.** In this area, we focus on the closest relationships they have, have lost, or someday want to have. This is where family reunification comes into play. *In most cases, people who find themselves in extreme poverty have burned a lot of bridges—and that is especially true for men.* Parents, spouses, children, siblings, and close friends have possibly all told them, "I'm done with you," or, "You can't be in our lives anymore." The relational rebuilding that needs to take place while restoring a broken life is something that requires a tremendous amount of help.

I have found that when kids are involved, these wounds run especially deep. Extreme reactions can take place in these very sensitive relationships. As a result of drug and alcohol abuse and a prison sentence, one man lost contact with his daughter, and his response upon release was to demand that he be back in her life without going through the restorative processes necessary for that to happen in a legal and healthy way. Another lost contact with his daughter due to drug and alcohol abuse and the relationship with her mother breaking down, and his response was to believe the lie that maybe his daughter was better off without him. Both examples are of typical and highly emotional responses that will need relational attention, so be prepared.

The restorative process has to engage these relationships that have been torn apart if there is any chance of experiencing reconciliation and reunification. We do believe in working with married men and women and will consider allowing limited contact in those relationships in Phase 2, whereas new romantic relationships are not allowed until Phase 3. For those who are married and entering a restorative process, a good portion of their deep pain and heartbreak has likely come from what they did or said to their spouse or from what their spouse did or said to them. Please note, it is important to gauge any levels of codependency and/or toxicity. There is no way to engage their restorative process without working through how these relationships are impacting them, because even if the other person isn't present in their life physically, it does not mean the person isn't still present in their hearts and minds daily.

In the Restoration Program, the primary tool in the relational belt is counseling. We are blessed to have a Licensed Professional Counselor (LPC), and oftentimes, we have counseling interns from local universities who work privately with the men and women and take the time to dig into those relational heart wounds in a confidential setting. The LPC analyzes family trees to help them understand if destructive cycles in their lives likely have been generational in their families. This provides insight as to why the same struggles and situations have continued to bring broken relationships and poverty.

The men and women do sign a Release of Information (ROI), allowing the counselor to talk with key chaplains should there be anything that might hinder their participation in the program. Thankfully, the times the LPC and chaplains collaborate in those types of cases are rare, and the program men and women feel very free to open up in the counseling environment in virtually every case. We've seen that men and women coming out of extreme poverty often have aspects of their story so personal and traumatic that they will not share them in a class, group, or even a chaplain/pastor meeting. In most cases, the counseling environment is the best setting for repressed and deep trauma to be processed. If you cannot afford to have an LPC on staff, then attempt to find volunteer counselors or budget for those you serve to receive counseling, and require it.

In the relational area, some of the other benchmarks we restore include:

- **Good Dads**. This is a state-certified class that helps men learn how to be better dads, and even advocates for them in family court and with child support enforcement.

- **Within My Reach**. This is also a state-certified class in the same program as Good Dads and is primarily focused on healthy romantic relationships.

- ***Unwanted: How Sexual Brokenness Reveals Our Way to Healing* by Jay Stringer**. A book that helps men find healing from the pain of sexual trauma and shame of sexual sin, and equips them to overcome lust and addiction to pornography.

- ***Boundaries* by Henry Cloud and John Town-send.** This book helps both men and women learn how to say no and to protect themselves from code-pendency and other toxic relational tendencies that are common in addiction, criminal life, and genera-tional poverty.

- **Social Capital.** We ask the men and women to reach out and develop as many relationships as possible in the community so that when they graduate, their cir-cle of influence is greater than just us.

- **Community Impact**. There are a required number of service and outreach event-type projects that help teach how important it is to have a relationship with their community.

***PERSONAL.*** This is the area most would refer to as "case management," which I would describe as helping someone take care of the most practical areas of their life. If God knows the number of hairs on our head and a sparrow doesn't fall from the sky without Him knowing (see Luke 12:6–7), then it is clear He is interested in the details of our lives. One prac-tical area of restoring lives is seen in watching men find financial relief from having so much garnished from their check that they are tempted to just give up and go back to their old life. In dozens of cases so far, many men keep work-ing, pressing forward, and paying far more child support in the end than if they had quit and run again.

The chaos and insecurity that come with substance abuse

or homelessness lead to men and women losing their most basic personal documents, and even reentering society from incarceration, it is common for them not to have their state ID, birth certificate, and/or Social Security card. We require all three by the end of Phase 1. There are resources in our community that provide funding and systems to help those unemployed or just released from jail and prison to get ID and birth certificates. I encourage you to take the time to access the resources for these personal needs of the people you serve. If you don't have the time initially, then at least create a list of these resources as you come across them.

Another sad example we see that illustrates how necessary it is to pursue wholistic restoration comes in this personal area. Making certain that they have a valid driver's license and the title, registration, and insurance for the car, and all in their name, is not something that is always seen to be necessary for those who are coming out of extreme poverty. More than one of our program participants has left or been removed because they did not want to wait to drive until they were legally ready to do so. Even if many things are going well in the other four areas, it would only take one ticket and parole violation, or worse, an accident and judgment for damages, for things to go bad. *Do not overlook what seem to be the most obvious legal and ethical areas of their personal lives.*

Because of the entry requirements for the learning environments throughout the program, most of our men and women have either their high school diploma, GED, or HiSet. If not, we require that. We use other things as benchmarks in the personal area of restoration, including:

- **Vision board.** We provide construction paper and

hundreds of old magazines for clippings and encourage them to express themselves however they want to create a visual reminder and representation of what they are working toward.

- **Legal issues.** Two-thirds of our men are on probation or parole (P&P), so we have developed a close partnership with our local P&P office and now have a designated P&P officer to help them satisfy their state supervisory obligations.

- **Health coverage.** Our community has a free health care option for those who don't have Medicaid. We developed a partnership with a local MD. We teach that the ER is for emergencies only, because medical bills set back restoration.

- **SMART goals.** These goals are Specific, Measurable, Achievable, Relevant, and Time-bound.

- **Classes.** We have an assortment of life skills and restoration classes that cover things like communication, goal setting, diet and nutrition, and scheduling.

- **Personal hygiene.** We speak into how they present themselves: how often they shower, what kind of clothing they wear, the importance of being shaven and combed, not wearing their hats crooked or backward, etc. We make sure to teach what all this communicates to the people around them.

- **Personal cleanliness.** This focuses on living space,

clutter and hoarding, not doing laundry enough, falling short on chores, etc.

- **Library card.** We ask them to get a card and learn how to utilize the library.

*VOCATIONAL.* We do not allow work outside of the program during Phase 1, which is approximately three months. One of the most common questions we get when interviewing someone for the program is, "So you're saying I can't go to work for at least three months?" To which our wholistic restoration-inspired response is, "No, we're going to go right to work—on your core life-controlling issues that a job hasn't solved yet."

Phase 1 is designed to focus on helping them become a good candidate that can not only get a job and keep a job, but also thrive in, be satisfied by, and glorify God in that job. The primary curriculum for their vocational restoration is one already mentioned, Jobs for Life (JfL)—a biblically based and community partnership-building approach to preparing people for the workforce. I cannot recommend it enough. Check to see if your community already has someone offering JfL to whom you can send your program participants. If not, becoming certified to offer JfL is a bit of a process, but don't let that deter you. It is more than worth the time and financial resources.

Like in the relational area, there are a lot of vocational bridges that have almost surely been burned, and work histories with mainly short-term jobs, large gaps without employment, and many terminations. If you are in a small community, that reality will make for a long list of what JfL calls roadblocks. It is impossible to overestimate the importance of giving close attention to restoring the vocational area of their lives. I would like to share a couple of extremes in this area to be aware of.

First, there are those you will serve who never had a strong work ethic taught to or modeled for them. It won't be easy for them to get to an employee-of-the-month status in just a few short months. You will be tempted to view them as irresponsible and need to take into account that there is more work to be done in this area for them than for most people. At Victory Mission + Ministry, we are blessed to have paid internships that can give extended time for workforce development. You may have to extend their Phase 1 and implement some weeks of intensive workforce readiness training. This, of course, is if the person is willing and doing the best they can, not if the person is putting out little effort and avoiding work.

Second, there are those you will serve who find their identity in work. We say over and over that Phase 1 is to work on healing their past hurts and addressing their core life-controlling issues, yet some participants' minds are consumed with counting the days until they can finally get a job. *If someone's identity is in their work, they could likely push back on policies that restrict where and when they can work.* We now restrict both second and third shifts, and we limit their work weeks to a maximum of fifty hours. We don't allow work on most day-labor job sites due to the unstable nature, lack of tax withholding, and likelihood of drug exposure in that kind of work environment. We restrict jobs in food service that serve alcohol. The purpose of these types of restrictions is to help them remain focused on their restorative process.

I would like to address third shifts, or what are often called overnight or graveyard shifts. We have always restricted third shifts in the Restoration Program. There was a time when one of our most lovable young men was going into Phase 3, and he had an opportunity for higher pay if he took that shift. He asked for an exception, and I told him no. I told him, as they learn in JfL, we are made for work but not made to work, and that there is more to life than work and money. When we are asleep while everyone else is awake, and awake while everyone else is asleep, we see relationships suffer, church involvement decrease, nutrition and exercise routines fall off, personal details in life get overlooked, and depression or anxiety follow. He was not receptive to accepting that restriction, so he left the program. He relapsed and found a couple of the deep truths from the teachings of Jesus manifest in his life: "For what does it profit a man to gain the whole world and forfeit his soul?" and, "One's life does not consist in the abundance of his possessions." (see Mark 8:36 and Luke 12:15b).

More benchmarks in the vocational area of life are:

- **Experience and skills.** We find out early what past work experience our participants have and if they have any certifications or skills that make them marketable in a field of work. This helps in referring them to potential jobs that you may come across.

- **Vocational dreams.** Jobs for Life has a process for the creation of a long-term vocational plan. In short, we want to know what their dreams are. Some want to start businesses, become substance abuse counselors, gain a trade certification, etc.

- **Volunteer assignments.** We not only designate them to twenty hours per week of volunteering in Phase 1, but we also evaluate their performance and help them learn and grow through their time of volunteering.

- **MO Job Center**. It is a requirement that they register at our state-run employment service, which offers various job fairs. Some of the training is also worth participants' time.

*FINANCIAL.* Last, but certainly not least, is money. *The area where you will find the second-most amount of resistance in your monitoring and restricting is their money* (the first is romantic relationships). After the kingdom of God, money—including wealth and possessions—was Jesus' most frequently taught topic, so we should not avoid it. Without question, the most effective and beneficial thing we have done in this area of their restorative process is structuring the Phase 2 financial requirements. We call it 10-20-30-40. In the phase where they begin working, they begin giving and paying and saving, not just spending. The 10% is the tithe to their home church. The 20% is their program fee. The 30% is the amount we save for them. The 40% they keep with chaplain approval for any significant expenditures. This has been a game-changer for them. We have heard: "I've never had $100, much less over $1,000 in a savings account. Heck, I've never even had a bank account." "Where did all my money used to go if I can live on 40% after room and board?" "Somehow I don't even miss that 10% that goes to my church." If you have ever worked with people in extreme poverty, those are huge paradigm shifts, and you have to make your financial policies highly structured at first for the lessons to be easily learned and long-lasting.

One of our favorite stories in this area is about a man who came to us after serving seventeen straight years in prison. On his first day in Restoration, he had no possessions or savings, but he had a determination to do whatever he had to do to build a life. He saved enough money not only to buy a car in Phase 3, but also to buy a house that he moved into upon graduating from the program. Another one of our graduates had the mother of his kids resisting his reentering their life. As a wholistically restored man with good financial discipline, he was able to save enough to afford the attorney he needed to increase how much time he spent with his kids. This will be a hard area to press on in their life, but don't let the difficulty tempt you to leave their financial lives unaddressed and unrestored.

Some of the other financial benchmarks we measure include:

- **Financial freedom.** There is a Phase 1 class that covers the important basics of banking and financial systems, predatory lending, etc.

- **Bank accounts.** We require them to set up both checking and savings accounts. A large majority of those below the poverty line are unbanked.

- **Savings verification**. Monthly, and sometimes randomly, we require them to verify how much is in their personal savings account.

- **Savings goals.** This is always required to be a SMART (Specific, Measurable, Achievable, Relevant, Time-bound) goal.

- **Budget.** An accurate budget must be presented and approved before transitioning to the next phase in the program.

- **Credit score.** Many landlords, and even employers, are checking credit scores, so we help them get theirs and work to improve their score.

- **Residential transition.** We expect $2,000 in our program participants' savings accounts to cover all the expenses of moving out of Phase 3 housing upon graduating.

These are only a small sample of a much larger and growing list of benchmarks we are tracking through our participants' process toward wholistically restored lives. I encourage you not to let the number of benchmarks overwhelm you. Feel free to visit www.changeforthepoor.org and reach out to me if you would like to receive the full list of benchmarks in all five wholistic areas. It can seem like a lot of box-checking, but they truly are vital for leading those you serve into a wholistically restored life—a life that John 10:10 describes as full and abundant. That is the kind of life Jesus came to make available to us.

# Chapter Eight Notes

# CHAPTER NINE

# Raising the Bar

*Everyone then who hears these words of mine and does them will be like a wise man who built his house on the rock. And the rain fell, and the floods came, and the winds blew and beat on that house, but it did not fall, because it had been founded on the rock. And everyone who hears these words of mine and does not do them will be like a foolish man who built his house on the sand. And the rain fell, and the floods came, and the winds blew and beat against that house, and it fell, and great was the fall of it.*

**—Matthew 7:24–27**

We had a man come into town, off of a bus and straight to the program, who was trying to recover from massive marijuana use and suffering from major depression, anxiety, and bouts of paranoia. He was the poster boy for the hippie life—dreadlocks and everything. I thought, "Oh my goodness, what are we going to do with this guy." But he was broken and willing, and we gave him a shot. He had a powerful encounter with God in the prayer courtyard and started leveling out by weeks number two and three.

Turns out, he is a master gardener and not a bad chef to boot. The community partnership in our city has a garden project, and they decided to partner with us to plant a garden at the shelter where our program and homeless men reside. While in Phase 2 and 3, our hippie who almost didn't make it through the first week of the program developed what became the crown jewel of our city's community gardens. After graduation, he took a job leading the kitchen and garden here that feed hundreds of people a day. Who knew? Truth is, I didn't know all those months before that the mess sitting in front of me was going to transform as completely as he did. *Every person sitting in front of us who looks like a big hot mess has God-given potential that the restorative process can unlock and unleash.*

It took a lot of experience working with people in extreme poverty for me to realize that in large part, individuals, churches, and organizations expect very little out of people who find themselves without any material or relational resources. It is easy to see that they are broke in terms of material and financial resources, and on the inside experiencing brokenness too, but we cannot forget that the imprint of God is on them. Also in them are unique gifts, talents, and abilities. I have found that when I increase my expectations of those I am serving, those who want to change rise to the occasion. Too often, we limit the amount of wholistic restoration in those we work with, because we limit our expectations of what they can and will do, which naturally limits what we ask of them.

Jesus closed out His most famous sermon with the passage quoted at the beginning of this chapter. He said that those who had just heard arguably the most difficult teaching in human history and put it into practice would have the foundation for living a life in the kingdom of God. The implications of a text like this are important. One implication of Matthew 7:24–27 is that building our foundation on the Rock is possible, and Jesus has an expectation that His followers are going to practice what He preached. I will admit that I often underestimate people coming off the streets and out of prison who have spent years, or even decades, in addiction, abuse, homelessness, crime, and more. The fact remains, however that every person we serve has untapped potential and purpose from God. I challenge you to raise the bar in your heart and mind of what those you serve are capable of. We won't see what God sees in them until we raise our expectations.

One way we raise the bar is through the intentionality put into our Phase 3 spiritual requirements. What I mean by "intentional" is that they are carefully structured to contain what most who know their Bible would consider a baseline of spiritual disciplines and practices necessary to live out the Christian faith. We tell the men going into Phase 3 housing that what is being asked of them spiritually is what we do in our lives as chaplains, some of us decades into our walk with God. Jesus asks us to put all of His teachings into practice, not just for a season of life, but for the rest of our lives. In the Great Commission, in addition to telling them to baptize and remember He would always be with them, Jesus included: "...teaching them to obey all that I have commanded you" (Matthew 28:20a). *The final phase of requirements in your restorative process should begin to resemble what it looks like for someone to remain a faithful follower of Jesus Christ.*

While back on staff at the church, when we were rolling

out the restorative program we called the Life Change Plan, I would regularly make my rounds to the groups and classes to update them on our progress—things we were learning and changes we were making. One of those presentations was in a Sunday school class of mostly older ladies, which was one of my favorites. After I rolled out all the requirements we would expect from the men and women signing up for the Life Change Plan, one lady looked at my handout, looked at me, looked at my handout, and then looked at me again and said, "Unless I am missing something, these requirements for your recovery people look like what all of us should be doing."

I didn't really know how to respond at that moment, but I knew she was right. What would seem like a raising of the bar to multitudes of regular American churchgoers is actually what Jesus has laid down for all of His followers to be doing, no matter how far along they are in their faith. When you are leading a restorative process or program, you have an opportunity to redefine discipleship for those you are serving and to build lives with their foundation on the Rock. You have an opportunity to teach that the sort of Christianity marked by attending a Sunday service two to three times a month, giving from what is left over, serving when time allows, reading the Bible sporadically through the week, and praying primarily in moments of need is a life with its foundation built on the sand.

Besides the more spiritual areas of life, we also raise the bar in other ways. Using a transitional approach in our Phase 1, 2, and 3 process, we hand off personal responsibility and freedoms to our men and women throughout their time in the Restoration Program. You might be surprised to see how impactful it is when trust and responsibility are given to someone coming out of addiction, jail or prison, homelessness, etc. Over the years, they begin to feel like they can no longer be trusted with anything valuable. A benefit of the phasing approach is that after some time with high levels of structure and accountability, they can begin to earn your trust for certain benefits and privileges. When that happens, they see themselves as having value, potential, and worth for the first time in their lives.

We see this in giving the keys to our ministry vehicle to the participant who has a valid driver's license and a clean driving record. We also see this in our organization when paid internships are given to Phase 2 men and women. The paid interns are given supervisory duties over volunteers and interaction with the public, including donors, partner organizations, etc. Raising the bar is a game-changer, trust me. *You may be the first person or church or organization to believe in them for a very long time, if ever.*

There are people in extreme poverty waiting for someone to see in them what they do not see in themselves, and you can be that "someone." But first, what kind of bar have you set for yourself? Is it as high as it should be? I have a vision of large numbers of individuals, churches, and organizations applying these restoration principles at some level, and new, trained and certified Restoration Programs launching across the country. If that is going to happen, a lot of restoration leaders will have to raise the bar for themselves. For those who identify as followers of Jesus, raising the bar could have significant implications on the five wholistic areas of their life. Should we not be bold and transparent in what we expect of ourselves, and not only of those we are leading through the restorative process? I suggest that this would greatly increase their respect for and trust in us as leaders.

I'd like to challenge you to raise the bar and believe God can do more in and through your life and ministry than you may think in this moment or season of your life. One thing that has held me back is a lack of confidence in what God has put in me by way of gifting and calling. I almost talked myself out of writing this book! I remember fighting people back in 2011 who were trying to get me to start preaching and teaching. More recently, I was hesitant to take a higher leadership role in restoration ministry here at Victory Mission + Ministry.

*I believe that Satan's best tactics include getting us to settle for less, lower the bar, and cut off at the knees the impact our ministries can have in the lives of people.* The Bible says, "For we are his workmanship, created in Christ Jesus for good works, which God prepared beforehand, that we should walk in them" (Ephesians 2:10). If you have heard God's call on your life to restorative ministry, if this has been confirmed by trusted people you are close with, and if evidence has also confirmed it in some way while you serve, then stop talking yourself out of your potential impact!

# Chapter Nine Notes

# CHAPTER TEN

# Include the Innkeeper

*But a Samaritan, as he journeyed, came to where he was, and when he saw him, he had compassion. He went to him and bound up his wounds, pouring on oil and wine. Then he set him on his own animal and brought him to an inn and took care of him. And the next day he took out two denarii and gave them to the innkeeper, saying, "Take care of him, and whatever more you spend, I will repay you when I come back."*

**—Luke 10:33–35**

In the famous Good Samaritan parable, there is an unsung and lesser-known hero in the story: the innkeeper. One of my favorite innkeepers for the Restoration Program is our local Probation and Parole (P&P) office. In a residential program where many of those involved are on state supervision, it can be very challenging to work with different directives from different P&P officers. Through our building a relationship with our P&P office, they decided to assign one P&P officer to supervise all of the men in the Restoration Program. This officer comes to see the men instead of them having to make their way to his office, which in the early stages of the program is difficult due to the high restrictions and lack of transportation.

The P&P officer assigned to us is truly their champion throughout the process. He comes to most of our celebrations and graduations. He appears in court with the men who are doing very well in the program to advocate for them. The men who come in from jail and prison are blown away by this. I am not saying by and large that other P&P offices and officers do not care or that they do not build relationships with those they supervise. What I am saying is that the investment we have made in making P&P an innkeeper for our program has improved our participants' lives in measurable and immeasurable ways.

Presumably, even though the compassionate Samaritan was paying for the expenses it would take to care for the man he found beat up and in a ditch, it is reasonable to believe that the innkeeper did not have to take the man in. However, he did, and in doing so, he became a crucial partner in the restorative process for the broke and broken man in the story. I hope you've picked up on my use of the word *innkeeper* in this illustration as synonymous with *partner*. We are compiling more and more innkeepers in the Restoration Program, and more than a handful are what I would consider key partnerships. These innkeepers improve and intensify the restorative experience for every man and woman participating. *Innkeepers have the potential to make an especially big impact because they bring supplemental resources to the table that you do not have available or do not have the experience and expertise to provide.*

Here are a few things to remember when searching for

potential innkeepers, or partnerships. First, make sure they align with your philosophy of ministry. We have church partnerships across the spectrum of evangelical Christianity and some partnerships that are not even faith-based organizations, so this is not about getting into the weeds of theological and denominational divisions. Being as inclusive as you can with your partnerships is a good thing, but be careful when considering partnerships with those whose beliefs and teachings are significantly different than yours. One example of that would be a partner that approaches helping with a relief-based mindset, as opposed to your restoration-based mindset; at the very least, that could be confusing to those you are serving.

Second, make sure they aren't one-way partnerships. I realize there is no such thing, by the way: as soon as it is one-way, it isn't a partnership. I have noticed in business and ministry that *partnering* is a buzzword these days. And people who want to do things on the quick or find people and organizations to do the heavy lifting for their vision may ask you to "partner" with them. Ask yourself: what are they bringing to the table in the partnership? Do they seem to be overly focused on getting a platform with those you're serving without much of a real contribution on the whole? Are they name-dropping you so they can get better publicity in the community?

Third, look for administratively friendly partnerships. In other words, does the work that the partnership creates for your staff and volunteers outweigh or overshadow the potential benefit to your men and women? An example of this would be a counselor who wants to volunteer their time but is thirty minutes away and cannot come to you. While that offer to donate professional time in and of itself is very valuable and appealing, it is likely that the human and financial resources required to make it happen are not cost-effective for you.

I would like to highlight another innkeeper that fits a need for us. Regarding the need to process through addictions and deep hurts, we have a Christ-centered twelve-step program called Living Free. Living Free (LF) is in some ways similar to the well-known Celebrate Recovery (CR) program birthed by Rick Warren's Saddleback Church. If you have the budget and people-power in your church or organization, by all means, get trained up and run one of these internally. However, if unlimited budgets and volunteers do not describe your current situation, see if one of these classes is offered locally and have your men and women complete it as a requirement. Outside of this curriculum category, countless programs exist that can help us caregivers remain on the front lines more and in the curriculum-writing business less.

We cannot encourage you enough to cultivate good relationships with the leaders of your partner organizations, because they likely know people who could help open doors in many ways for your program. *Innkeepers spread your restoration stories by the most effective and least expensive method there is: word of mouth.* If those you are serving are experiencing true restoration in their lives, their stories get told in the partner organizations and the circles of influence of those volunteering, and beyond. We are receiving more and more media attention that leads to applications, referrals ,and donations. We hear of members from a church partner telling one of our restoration stories, which led to one of our guys getting a great job offer. People are captivated by stories of dramatic life change. They grip us, so much so that we love them in movies and books when we know they aren't real. When there is real-life change for the poor, that story is even more compelling. Therefore, every innkeeper is a storyteller.

Earlier in the book, we covered the danger of us as caregivers needing to be needed and finding our identity in this kind of work. An unintended result of this is developing unhealthy connections to those we serve. I have to confess to drifting into this mindset and practice if I am not careful. Luckily, the Holy Spirit and some really good leaders, prayer partners, and team members help keep this from getting out of control for me. I mention this again here because finding innkeepers can provide a great safeguard against drifting into codependent caregiver mode. When you become just one of many sources of leadership and influence for each participant in the restorative process, it creates a healthier environment for all involved.

Finally, I have found intentionality to be more key to cultivating innkeepers than time spent on this as a ministry task. When you see what the deepest needs of your burden demographic are, simply do some research and networking to find out what people and/or organizations in your community may be well suited to come alongside your participants. Once you have identified a potential innkeeper, reach out to them to set up a meeting and see if a partnership makes sense. Maintaining the health of the partnership with innkeepers can become organic if you stay in touch while doing the work of ministering to the same men and women, and keep organized by periodically scheduling meetings to evaluate how the partnership is going. The frequency of those check-in meetings for us ranges from quarterly to yearly, depending on how

intensively the innkeeper works with our program participants.

## Chapter Ten Notes

_____

_____

_____

_____

_____

_____

_____

_____

_____

_____

_____

_____

_____

_____

_____

_____

# Second Principle: Structure

1. Read Proverbs 3:5–8. Discuss how those in extreme poverty might be impacted by trusting God and/or your restorative process. What can you do to create or cultivate trust from those you serve?

_____

_____

_____

_____

_____

_____

_____

_____

_____

_____

_____

2. How can the realization, or reminder, that we have more time than we think (168 hours in a week) influence how you approach scheduling for those you serve?

_____

_____

_____

_____

_____

_____

_____

_____

_____

_____

3. Revisit the percentages at the end of Chapter Seven. Were you surprised to find how little one year is compared to the rest of your life? How might this change your mindset regarding restoration?

_____

_____

_____

_____

_____

_____

_____

_____

_____

_____

_____

4. What is your history or experience with SMART goals? Make at least one now.

_____

_____

_____

_____

_____

_____

_____

_____

_____

_____

_____

_____

5. Up to this point, has your personal or group effort to help those in extreme poverty been wholistic? Which of the five wholistic areas were missing, and why do you think they were?

_____

_____

_____

_____

_____

_____

_____

_____

_____

_____

_____

_____

6. In the description of wholistic areas, which benchmarks stood out to you, and why?

_____

_____

_____

_____

_____

_____

_____

_____

_____

7. How and when have you underestimated the potential in a person you attempted to help?

_____

_____

_____

_____

_____

_____

_____

_____

_____

_____

8. Take time to consider whether or not you need to raise the bar in what you believe you are capable of. What does living into what you believe God has called you to do look like?

_____

_____

_____

_____

_____

_____

_____

_____

_____

_____

9. Read Luke 10:25–37. Have you ever paid much attention to the innkeeper in the story? If so, how so? If not, why not?

_____

_____

_____

_____

_____

_____

_____

_____

10. What innkeepers have helped you and/or your group serve the poor? How did those partnerships work? Is there a partnership you need to quit, create, or cultivate right now?

_____

_____

_____

_____

_____

_____

_____

_____

_____

_____

# Third Principle of Restoration: Accountability

# You Did *What* with the Money?

*"Behold, I am sending you out as sheep in the midst of wolves, so be wise as serpents and innocent as doves."*
**—Matthew 10:16**

Years ago, I learned a hard lesson about how ineffective, or even harmful, it can be to give money to persons in poverty without any measure or system of accountability. It was when I was on staff at the church. One of the families in the church wanted to donate a car to one of the struggling families that came to the outreach service we started. I had the perfect match: a mom of two little ones working full-time and helping take care of her in-laws while her husband had trouble keeping a job. Every Sunday night, she would push the stroller down the street behind the church and through the parking lot to get her and those little ones to worship, and she would walk a good distance to the bus stop and ride the bus every day to and from work. I thought about what a blessing this would be for her and her family. I had some concerns about the dynamic of three out of four of the adults in the house not regularly working, but what could be wrong with giving a poor family a car, right?

Less than a month later, I was outside the back door on a Sunday night and there she came pushing her kids in the stroller to the service. I waited for her and frustratedly said, "Hey there, where is the car?" to which she replied embarrassedly, "I had to sell it to pay the electric bill."

Is the young, hard-working mom the "wolf," and I the "sheep," in the instruction Jesus gave in Matthew 10:16? Was she malicious, and I innocent? It may be tempting to think along these terms, but no, not at all. However, from this experience, I learned a couple of very valuable lessons. I learned that at the time, I lacked the wisdom to take in the whole situation and get involved in a way that would lead to a restorative outcome. I also learned how heartbreaking it is to watch the heartfelt gift of a good family not bring blessing to its intended recipient. Maybe I was as innocent as a dove, but I was definitely not as wise as a serpent. Regardless, I learned that *when serving those in extreme poverty, naiveté can cause people to get hurt*. Not only did the person who gave the car feel slighted, but also the woman who sold it felt ashamed.

To be clear, the accountability principle of restoration is about a lot more than just money and possessions, but that being such a huge area of their lives needing restoration, let's go ahead and start there. When giving money or material possessions to those in (or just coming out of) extreme poverty, there must be accountability to how the money is used or spent. In the restorative process, it is essential to have a spending limit that, if exceeded, requires approval beforehand and a receipt afterward. Even after the experience with the young mom selling the donated car to pay an electric bill, I still struggled with requiring that level of accountability for grown men and women in their financial lives, but it is imperative that we do so.

In the Restoration Program, participants in Phase 1 can only have up to $10 on them per week and are required to keep receipts for money spent. In Phase 2, purchases over $100 require approval and verification of major purchases, and bank account balances are required. For Phase 3, the amount requiring approval increases to $150, and regular verification of those purchases and bank account balances are also still required.

As I mentioned, I was a slow learner in this area of attempting to bring change for the poor. In the first months that I led the Restoration Program, there was little financial accountability for those in the program. In Phase 1, that fostered an environment of bartering food stamps for money from friends inside and outside the program, receiving and spending gifted money from enabling family members, purchasing lottery tickets, etc. That is some of what I know about, and I hope there wasn't anything worse. In Phase 2, program fees and required savings had not been implemented, so men were getting jobs and then eating out every night (even though we provided three meals a day), buying $900 electronic devices, and financing $15,000 vehicles from predatory lending car lots. Men and women who find themselves needing a long-term, wholistically restorative process are very likely not to have the life skill of wise financial management.

I plead with you: do not set yourself up for frustration, nor set back those you serve, by neglecting to implement measures of financial accountability. If you grew up in an environment where creditors weren't calling, evictions weren't being served, and government programs weren't being resourced for basic needs, then this may seem like overkill to you. I promise, it isn't. In fact, if you have the staff for it, I recommend having your restoration participants account for every dollar spent and, at least, randomly checking a month of their finances against their approved budget. The foundational discipline this sets up in their life will dramatically increase their chances for getting out and staying out of financial poverty.

You might be thinking that this sounds like not trusting the men and women in the restorative process, and didn't I just tell you to trust them with things? Fair question. First, increasing the amount requiring approval facilitates an environment of growing trust in them. But second, I believe in the restorative approach of the Russian proverb, "Trust but verify." *We are going to trust our participants with a growing amount of financial freedom through the restorative process but ask for verification along the way to hold them accountable.*

We will soon get into how to respond when a participant is defiant toward rules like this. However, when a well-known rule is broken or pushed back against, it shows a lack of trust in your leadership and the restorative process as a whole.

## Chapter Eleven Notes

# Peer Pressure

*...submitting to one another out of reverence for Christ.*
**—Ephesians 5:21**

We talk a lot about the need for men and women in the restorative process to submit to the leadership of the staff and certain volunteers. As we move further along, we will learn more about how that works and what it looks like. In this chapter, I would like to focus on another very powerful and important level of accountability: peer accountability. It is considered by some to be the *most* effective form of accountability. I am going to assume that if you have staff, each person works 40 to 50 hours per week. As we saw earlier, there are 168 hours in seven days of our week. Given a long work week of 50 hours, there are still well over 100 hours left every week when your men and women in the restorative process do not have direct supervision and guidance. Think about that. Over two-thirds of their time is spent without you in or near their presence. Given what we know about the lack of readiness to take on life and consistently make good choices, this poses significant risks and problems.

Peer supervision is a vital piece of the puzzle in the restorative process. The title of this chapter likely provokes thoughts of teenage years where we were all easily influenced by our friends to do bad things. However, peer pressure can be a positive thing. Even as adults, we tend to live differently around people we know are walking out a healthy life; and besides, as Christians, aren't we called to be our brother's keeper? Check this out in Genesis 4:8–9: "Now Cain said to his brother Abel, 'Let's go out to the field.' While they were in the field, Cain attacked his brother Abel and killed him. Then the LORD said to Cain, 'Where is your brother Abel?' 'I don't know,' he replied. 'Am I my brother's keeper?'"

We tell our men and women the answer to God's question to Cain is *yes*. Yes, we have a responsibility when it comes to watching out for each other. Instead of inviting his brother out to the fields for an ambush, Cain should have engaged Abel and asked for help in working through how to bring an offering pleasing to the Lord next time. Just like, in the story of their parents' first sin, Adam should have been there watching Eve's back and helping defend against the devastating lies of the serpent. One of the many things these biblical stories illustrate is the importance of being there for each other.

*On the streets and in jails and prisons, the culture is not one of watching each other's backs, at least in the way it is called for in a Christian community setting.* We ask our Residential Supervisors (RSs) to be their brother's keepers. We ask them to lead to whatever level they are capable while the staff is not present, and we remind them often that they should see themselves as "servant leaders." A challenge most RSs have is being asked to tell us when their peers are failing or struggling. Most of those you serve will initially consider that snitching, or ratting, or narcing (pronounced "narking"). Along with a multitude of many other attitudes you will have to address, this is an important mindset you will have to lovingly lead them to leave in their past.

We do ask them to follow the process Jesus laid out in Matthew 18 of going first to their brother or sister to find a resolution. If that does not lead to reconciliation, then they are to get another brother or sister to try to resolve things—in our case, two to three RSs. Then, if that does not align the wayward person with what the program is asking of them, the RS team brings that to staff. Indeed, in the end, if someone has broken significant rules, or has a serious struggle going on, the RS team will let them know that they do have to bring us into the loop so we can best minister to them; but, with the small stuff, we truly allow the peer leaders to lead. In our case, these peer leaders are called the RS team. In sober living homes, they are often referred to as house managers. In college dorms, they are still called RAs (resident assistants or advisors).

One of the most gut-wrenching examples of what it can cost to ask people in the restorative process to lead their peers came when one of our RSs had to tell us that his best friend in the program was talking with the girlfriend whom he was restricted from having contact with. You could see the heaviness it brought him to have to do it. It strained their friendship and started a chain of events that led to the other young man choosing to leave the program. Within a few short months, he overdosed and died. The RS, who did the right thing in that case, ended up graduating and is answering a call to pastoral ministry, confirmed by us and his home church. He knows that what he did was right, but I am sure he will always carry some amount of weight on his heart as a result. That may be an extreme example, but I share it to convey how difficult and challenging it can be for peers to lead their peers in a 24/7 residential environment. Do not underestimate how much attention you will need to give to nurturing these peer leaders. We provide what we call leadership development training (LDT) to train and build up our RS team.

*The LDT is a four-month process consisting of three main components: on the job training, book and video learning, and personal assessments.* On-the-job training is pretty self-explanatory, but in weekly meetings with trainees, we process their leadership and interactions with their peers in an action-reflection learning environment. Additionally, books are read and discussed monthly, and video training sessions are viewed and discussed weekly. Finally, each month, a personal assessment is taken and discussed so that a better understanding of how they are gifted and created by God can impact their life and leadership.

In the model of the ministry of Jesus, the peer leadership team can take the form of what the twelve disciples were to Jesus. I admit there are some differences in dynamics, but some similarities exist as well. The RS team works through structured LDT experience, but more than that, and arguably more importantly than that, they are with the chaplains a lot. They sit in on difficult conversations, interviews, and removals, and they spend time around ministry life and leadership as the need arises in the day-to-day work. Those unstructured hours are so valuable. They remind me of the times Jesus would be in a typical life situation with His twelve disciples around Him and then break into a teaching moment. In these times, the RSs develop trust in me and each other. They open up, and growth skyrockets in their lives.

It is hard to make a handbook out of that kind of leadership training, to be honest. I hope my description can give you enough information to make it fit your unique gifting, calling, and personality. The essence of this aspect of leading your peer leaders is to do as much as you can to keep proper boundaries in place as their leader but also spend regular time with them, genuinely, not always scripted or task- or outline-oriented.

Back to positive peer pressure. *There is a perspective and influence that will come from the peer leaders that cannot come from you.* While our Phase 3 participants are not officially considered peer leaders, when they come in on the weekends to mentor our Phase 1 participants, they bring a shared experience to the relationship that is very valuable. Some programs I have collaborated with ask their graduates to come back in and give their testimonies or to lead classes or devotions. That, too, is giving those in the restorative process a leadership presence and example from someone who has been in their same shoes. If you are starting up and do not have graduates, or women and men in a Phase 3 kind of place, then find people in your community who have been restored from a life of extreme poverty and ask them to come share their stories.

In a practical sense, this also keeps you from taking calls all hours of the day or night. A good peer leadership team can take care of more of the questions and issues that come up after hours than you might think. Those of us in the caregiving profession can feel the need to be involved at too detailed of a level in our ministries or organizations. With the peer leadership team taking care of things that they can do, we are free to do what we are called to do: lead ourselves, our teams, and our peer leaders.

# Chapter Twelve Notes

_____

_____

_____

_____

_____

_____

_____

_____

_____

_____

_____

_____

_____

_____

_____

_____

# Redefining Discipline

*It is for discipline that you have to endure. God is treating you as sons. For what son is there whom his father does not discipline? If you are left without discipline, in which all have participated, then you are illegitimate children and not sons. Besides this, we have had earthly fathers who disciplined us and we respected them. Shall we not much more be subject to the Father of spirits and live? For they disciplined us for a short time as it seemed best to them, but he disciplines us for our good, that we may share his holiness. For the moment all discipline seems painful rather than pleasant, but later it yields the peaceful fruit of righteousness to those who have been trained by it.*

**—Hebrews 12:7–11**

What a clear and redemptive description of discipline! This understanding of discipline will be highly important for you to communicate to those you are leading through the redemptive process. I say often that our rules, restrictions, and requirements are protective, not punitive. They are meant to correct, not to condemn. When we have to impose additional discipline, we use what we call Discipline and Restoration

(D&R) plans; so, even in writing the title, there is a reminder that we are not focused on punishing, but on restoring. It is not about condemning the attitudes, actions, or words themselves, but about putting protective measures in place for a season, to change the underlying reason for the behavior. I have seen D&R plans make or break someone in the restorative process.

D&R plans are not more than one page. They don't go into great detail, and they are supplemental to the regular program requirements of whatever phase they find themselves in. A typical D&R plan will begin with a paragraph explaining the reason for the discipline, continue with a dozen or so bullet points of what is being expected, and then close with dates and signatures. Receiving and walking out a D&R Plan is a character-building opportunity if they are willing to see it that way. For our purposes, it provides what we call a "heart-check" moment for them. By this I mean that their response to receiving a D&R plan will serve to reveal the posture of their heart toward the restorative process.

A good example would be when our men and women move past the restriction of not being allowed personal electronic devices. Most often, it is a phone, which provides access to their old friends, family, and the outside world in general. When we see misuse or overuse of electronic devices, we will ask them to give up their device again so it does not distract them from what they are there to do—restore their lives. In more than half of those cases, they have chosen to leave the program. It is unfortunate, for sure, but it is a heart-check moment. *We have learned that if they will not give up a phone for a few weeks, then there is no way they will do what it takes to complete a long-term restorative process.*

We had a man do very well throughout Phase 1—we even elevated him into peer leadership—but when he reached Phase 2, the job and the car and the phone captured his heart. He began to destabilize enough that I asked him to turn in his keys and phone except for when he was going to work, at work, and coming back from work. He was unable to submit to that D&R plan, so he packed up and left. It was sad; we all loved the guy. However, the spirit of independence remained in him at a profound level, and he did not see the harvest of righteousness and peace that would have come from accepting discipline.

Please know and resolve in your heart now that those you are leading will not always agree or understand why a rule, restriction, and requirement is in place or why they are being disciplined the way they are, and that is perfectly okay. I tell the men and women all the time, "I do not expect you to agree or even understand, but I do expect you to submit." There are some pretty funny sayings from the recovery world that fit that moment: "Remember, your best thinking got you here." "You didn't come in here on a winning streak." "How was *your* program working out for you?"

One sobering proverb puts it this way: "There is a way that seems right to a man, but its end is the way to death" (Proverbs 14:12). We are not always right, not even those of us leading. Look back at the passage from Hebrews. We know earthly parents are not perfect, but their discipline is still used by God to raise, form, shape, and prepare children for life. It is not necessary for you to be right in every disciplinary decision you make. Don't overthink that; you will get better with experience. What is far more important is the principle of their accepting your (protective and not punitive) discipline.

143

This is the evidence that they are committed to fully trusting the process, as we discussed in Chapter Six.

I look back on times when I was on staff at the church. Major decisions were made on more than a handful of occasions that directly affected me both personally and vocationally. Some of those I disagreed with, and I did not understand why my leadership was making them, but I will never forget those seasons of prayer and submission and how God grew my faith and leadership and my relationship with Him. *I was taught by the Holy Spirit, and good men and women, that you are not a Christian leader until you learn how to follow Christian leaders.* I will humbly admit that I turned out to be clearly wrong about some of the decisions they made, but to this day, I believe that regarding some of the decisions, I was right on the issue itself. I laugh about those in hindsight because before much time passed, I realized it really doesn't matter.

I should point out these were not doctrinal issues where I was asked to believe and teach heresies. These were the kinds of church issues and decisions that well-meaning Christians can and do disagree about. What mattered more to God than who was wrong or right was whether or not I would submit. Did I struggle in some cases? Yes. Did I have bad days and weeks fighting through what submission looked like in some of those cases? Yes. But in the end, when I submitted, I was blessed, the church was blessed, and God was glorified. In whatever job they find themselves, the ability to submit to supervisors, managers, and employers will set your participants up for success.

Two of our first ten full-program graduates were at the top on the list of time spent under individual D&R plans. I do not think that is a coincidence. I think if they had not received that discipline and spent the time in it allowing a deeper restorative work in their heart, they would not be the men they are today, and they both give testimony to that being true. One thing many of our graduates have said, in their own words, is that we could have asked anything of them and as long as it wasn't immoral, illegal, or unbiblical, they would have done it. I say the next as general statements, trusting you will be led by the Spirit to recognize exceptions to the rule, but when in doubt of whether or not to take a phone away, take it away. When in doubt of whether or not to extend a phase of the program, extend it. When in doubt of whether or not to restrict a romantic relationship, restrict it, for a season at least. When in doubt of whether or not to allow an overnight pass, don't allow it. *At the end of the day, at the end of their program, the growth they experience from learning how to receive protective discipline will bear more fruit than allowing whatever they are wanting in that moment or season.*

It has been a while since we discussed the first principle of restoration—relationship—so it is worth noting that discipline must be given in an atmosphere of love, conversation, and prayer. If you don't have time to sit down face to face and share a D&R plan with a participant, then wait until you can do so to implement it. Relationship supersedes everything in the restorative process.

# Chapter Thirteen Notes

_____

_____

_____

_____

_____

_____

_____

_____

_____

_____

_____

_____

_____

_____

_____

_____

# CHAPTER FOURTEEN

# Grace and Truth

*And the Word became flesh and dwelt among us, and we have seen his glory, glory as of the only Son from the Father, full of grace and truth. For from his fullness we have all received, grace upon grace. For the law was given through Moses; grace and truth came through Jesus Christ. No one has ever seen God; the only God, who is at the Father's side, he has made him known.*

**—John 1:14, 16–18**

One night, I stayed late to remove a man we had repeatedly worked with on a couple of areas of his wholistic restoration. He just kept falling far too short. Plus, we discovered that he went from not doing his weekly soulwork to falsifying the information on it. There were half a dozen RSs in the room, and I took the time just to let him know that he had given us no choice but to remove him and that we hated to have to make that decision, but we loved him and would make referrals to programs that might be a better fit. We asked if we could encourage him and pray over him. He said yes. The tears flowed, and there were hugs all around.

CHANGE FOR THE POOR

Though letting him go was heartbreaking, I felt that it was a beautiful picture of loving someone enough to let them go. I felt like it embodied the ministry of Jesus: an unwillingness to compromise on truth and the covenant commitment that had been badly broken, but a desire to treat the man in that moment like he was deeply loved and able to rebound from any setback. Now, this approach does not ensure that everyone will receive and accept discipline or removal well, but it is how we administer the grace and truth of Jesus Christ.

We mentioned benchmarks earlier when introducing and unpacking the five areas of wholistic restoration. We need to see certain progress being made, or else we will ask men and women to move on to another environment that better fits what they are looking for in a program—and that is okay. The man in the story above had reached a point where far too many benchmarks were not being met. We are not legalistic about this, however, and will not discipline or remove them for genuinely struggling. If those become a pattern, then of course we have to deal with the pattern, but on the whole, we believe that our benchmarks are more than reasonable expectations for a person seeking to forever leave their life of material and relational poverty behind.

As mentioned in a previous chapter, we use benchmarks in the restorative process. Every six weeks, we bring in the men and women to go over their benchmarks. These meetings give us restorative leaders concentrated relational time to listen actively and to administer grace and truth before discipline or removal is needed. This time will consist of at least one chaplain or chaplain's apprentice and possibly a peer leader or two. It can sometimes feel like box-checking, so we do what we can to stop often and ask them to speak from their heart. They might speak about a class they took, an experience they had in their home church, what it was like to complete one of their community impact requirements, etc. We ask for full written testimonies of the restoration that is happening in their life, areas of healing, and what forgiveness means to them. You may refer back to Chapter Eight for the abbreviated list of our Phase 1 benchmarks.

*In these benchmark meetings, we take the opportunity to dig a little bit deeper than we would in the much shorter and less focused interactions we have with them throughout an average week or month.* For example, if they have to go through SATOP to get their driver's license back, we will want to know in one of the early benchmark meetings how many hours and dollars they are looking at, with those SATOP requirements. Then we ask them to make a SMART goal and get it done as soon as possible. Before these benchmark meetings, a consultation will happen between staff and peer leadership regarding what we want to be sure to celebrate and what we want to challenge them to work on. The biggest mistake we have made and continually work to improve in these is the length of the meeting itself. Thorough benchmark meetings will take at least one hour, and the ones that determine the transition to the next phase should probably take up to two or more hours for most in your restorative process. Of course, the length of these meetings will depend on the number of benchmarks you evaluate in each of the five wholistic areas of restoration.

If you do not adopt something close to our structure, and take a different timeline and frequency for these types of meetings, that is okay; but whatever you do, I would advise you not to go short on these meetings. Most often, getting to

through the restorative process. Grace cannot be granted to those undermining the rules and thereby jeopardizing the effectiveness and culture of your restorative process. In that case, it is not grace at all; instead, it becomes enabling someone who refuses, at least at that point in time, to take charge of restoring their lives.

The scripture that comes to mind here is, "Clothe yourselves, all of you, with humility toward one another, for 'God opposes the proud but gives grace to the humble'" (1 Peter 5:5b). In his epistle, James also refers to this truth, which is taken from both the Psalms and Proverbs in the Old Testament. When your participant becomes proud and defiant, then your grace becomes ineffective at best and destructive at worst. We must allow those we serve to make their choices and experience the consequences of those choices.

# Chapter Fourteen Notes

_____

_____

_____

_____

_____

_____

_____

_____

_____

_____

_____

_____

_____

_____

_____

CHAPTER FIFTEEN

# They're in Charge

*And as he (Jesus) was setting out on his journey, a man ran
up and knelt before him and asked him, "Good Teacher,
what must I do to inherit eternal life?" And Jesus said to him,
"Why do you call me good? No one is good except God
alone. You know the commandments: 'Do not murder, Do
not commit adultery, Do not steal, Do not bear false wit-
ness, Do not defraud, Honor your father and mother.'" And
he said to him, "Teacher, all these I have kept from my
youth." And Jesus, looking at him, loved him, and said to
him, "You lack one thing: go, sell all that you have and give
to the poor, and you will have treasure in heaven; and come,
follow me." Disheartened by the saying, he went away sor-
rowful, for he had great possessions.*
**—Mark 10:17–22**

Vance Havner, in his book *Jesus Only,* taking from a quote
attributed to many preachers and theologians, writes that
"the same sun melts ice and hardens clay, and the Word of
God humbles or hardens the human heart".[10] I love how that
describes our roles in leading people through the restorative
process. Spiritually speaking, of course, there is a direct

correlation. However, even in the other areas of wholistic restoration, the principle holds true. *We teach, we guide, we counsel, we correct, but we cannot make decisions for those we are serving.* As the old saying goes, you can lead a horse to water, but you can't make it drink. I think we know this intellectually, but I have also seen and experienced how we become personally and emotionally invested in the men and women we lead. Our wanting change for them can reach a level where we have a really hard time having the conversations, enforcing the rules, and implementing the discipline that we know they need to have because doing so may prompt them to choose to leave.

Jesus faced this dilemma in the passage above. He knew the young man's heart, and what it was that he clung so tightly to that if asked to give it up, he likely would not. After a long enough time with someone in an intense restorative process, you likewise tend to find out what things or people in their life they need to give up. When that thing or person begins to rise in prominence and priority over the restorative process, you have been put in a position of leadership to bring them to a place where they have to make a difficult choice. Then you have to do the very difficult part as a caregiver and allow them to make that choice and experience the consequences. The landmark book *Boundaries* by Henry Cloud and John Townsend lays out in great detail the biblical foundation for this philosophy of life and ministry.[11] I believe that allowing those we serve to experience the consequences of their choices is the make-or-break factor for fostering an environment where a person in extreme poverty can be wholistically restored.

One of my vocational mentors came to train our chaplain

team recently and captivated us with the phrase that I used for the title of this chapter: "They're in charge." It is their program. They can engage it as a covenant to which they must submit, where they are not the leader but the follower; and if they do so, they will be restored by it. Or they can manipulate it, which most often works itself out in one of a couple of ways: they get out of it what they can and leave when they get what they came for, or they conform superficially to the program but remain unchanged at the core level of who they are, until they are found out and removed. All of this is up to them, not you or me. We must allow them to make that choice.

If you think about it, this is how it works with us and following Jesus. We can walk through the narrow gate and onto the hard way that leads to life, or through the wide gate and onto the easy way that leads to destruction (see Matthew 7:13–14). Why would this principle not hold true in facilitating change for the poor?

The reality that they're in charge is not something to keep a secret, either. One roadblock for many in extreme poverty is the feeling of powerlessness. Fatalism—the mindset that the way things are is the way they will always be—pervades within generational poverty. "So why should I even try to escape my situation? Isn't this just my lot in life? Isn't this is the hand I've been dealt?" Teaching men and women with this mindset that they now have the resources at their disposal to change their life radically is empowering, to say the least. It may take a while in the process for them to embrace and take ownership of this truth, but don't give up emphasizing that they're in charge.

Let me say, even after deciding for discipline or removal

hundreds of times now, it is still not easy. I hope it never becomes easy for you, but I know this: *if you choose to make a practice of bailing men and women out of the consequences of their choices, you will not have a restorative environment, but chaos instead*—and the ones you are trying to save will end up leaving, anyway. Furthermore, the time they remain will set an example and lower the bar for those who want to do whatever it takes to be restored. Are you willing to let go of the ones who aren't ready to be wholistically restored? Are you ready to accept a handful of lives being dramatically and forever changed over the possibility of impacting multitudes of lives at levels that don't break cycles of material and relational poverty? If not, I suggest you pursue serving in an organization or ministry that employs the relief approach. I don't mean to be harsh in saying that; it could be you are more gifted to meet immediate needs caused by more situational circumstances in the lives of those you serve. However, I believe if you have made it to the end of this book, it is more likely that you are called to walk the long road of restoring lives with those in extreme poverty due to cyclical and/or generational causes.

Now let's explore some next steps. If you are working individually with people in extreme poverty and want to start by applying some of these principles, that is great. If you are someone involved in a church or organization that wants to apply these principles to an existing outreach program or mercy ministry, that is also great. For both of those scenarios, I wish you well, and Lord, hear our prayers for your restorative efforts. One thing you could consider is applying for a one-year chaplain apprenticeship with Victory Mission + Ministry. This experience would immerse you in the

Restoration Program and prepare you for leadership at a possible future satellite site launched by us, or for going back to start or lead a restorative ministry in your individual life, church, or organization. If, after reading and discussing this book, your church or organization is interested in launching something very similar to the Restoration Program we have at Victory Mission + Ministry, we would invite a conversation about that.

Thank you for your time in reading *Change for the Poor*. For more information about, or to explore how best to implement, any or all of these restorative principles and processes, please visit changeforthepoor.org. I am truly thankful to God for every person who may be impacted by doing the hard work of restoring lives with those in extreme poverty.

# Chapter Fifteen Notes

_____

_____

_____

_____

_____

_____

_____

_____

_____

_____

_____

_____

_____

_____

_____

_____

_____

# Third Principle: Accountability

1. Have you ever given someone money or material possessions only to find out later it got used for something you did not want it to be used for? If so, what was that experience like?

_____

_____

_____

_____

_____

_____

_____

_____

2. What financial policies do you have in place for those you serve? Do you need to decrease the amount they keep and increase verification? (refer to the 10-20-30-40 policy in Chapter Eight).

_____

_____

_____

_____

_____

_____

_____

_____

_____

3. Read Genesis 4:1–12. How does this story inform the idea of being our "brother's keeper?"

_____

_____

_____

_____

_____

_____

_____

_____

_____

_____

4. Do you have a peer leadership team and training in place right now? If so, how is it going? If not, what would it look like to create that?

_____

_____

_____

_____

_____

_____

_____

_____

_____

5. Read Hebrews 12:7–11. What does this passage say about the importance and purpose of discipline?

_____

_____

_____

_____

_____

_____

_____

_____

_____

6. Be honest—how difficult is it for you to discipline those you are trying to help escape extreme poverty? What would have to change for you to begin to do that?

_____

_____

_____

_____

_____

_____

_____

_____

_____

_____

7. After reading Chapter Fourteen, has your understanding of giving grace to those you serve changed? If so, how? If not, why not?

_____

_____

_____

_____

_____

_____

_____

_____

_____

_____

_____

8. If "the same sun that melts the ice hardens the clay" is true, then how might that take the pressure off of you as a leader of those in extreme poverty?

_____

_____

_____

_____

_____

_____

_____

_____

_____

9. How does the idea that "they're in charge" sit with you? Please give that serious thought.

_____

_____

_____

_____

_____

_____

_____

_____

_____

_____

the truth cannot be rushed. Also, unless you are ministering to a very small number, this is a unique time for them to feel valued by the focused and intentional time with their leaders. This lends itself to being an effective time to speak the truth in an environment already saturated with grace. In one of these meetings recently, I noticed—with the help of some of the peer leaders—that the man we were benchmarking would constantly compliment people and deprecate himself. I am not sure how I had missed that pattern in the first twelve weeks, but it was certainly there. We addressed it head-on, discerning that it was a long-held pattern of deflection and distraction for him. In a unique directive, I told him during Phase 2 he could not compliment his leaders. Directives like that may seem a little nitpicky, but they aren't, because they usually reveal something deeper is going on under that surface behavior. We will look closely at how important it is to make the hard choices to discipline and, at times, remove men and women.

In closing this chapter, I would like to address an objection to our restorative approach, one commonly held in both secular and faith-based approaches to poverty alleviation. Many people working with those in extreme poverty would categorize the restorative approach put forward in this book as being short on grace—the idea being, shouldn't we expect some failure from those in a restorative process? Doesn't it lack grace to just give up on someone? Isn't there some way to respect the rules while also allowing space for people to fail and receive grace? The answer is that *there is grace for seasons of genuine struggle combined with incremental change.* However, grace does not apply to defiance of the known and agreed-to rules, which reveals a lack of willingness to work

APPENDIX A

# Criteria for Participation

*And he [Jesus] said to all, "If anyone would come after me,
let him deny himself and take up his cross daily and follow
me. For whoever would save his life will lose it, but whoever
loses his life for my sake will save it. For what does it profit
a man if he gains the whole world and loses or forfeits himself?"*

**—Luke 9:23–25**

How do we evaluate whether or not someone is ready to
be in charge of all that is involved in completing a twelve- to
eighteen-month restorative process? In our handbook, we
have a description of who the *Restoration Program* is for: this
program is for anyone seeking to overcome life-controlling issues, including but not limited to addictions, codependency,
unhealed hurts, criminal thinking, generational poverty,
hopelessness, etc., through a Christ-centered approach that
focuses on faith-based restoration. We are looking for three
things that we believe will reveal to us if the man or woman is
seeking to overcome one or more of those life-controlling issues. Those three things are readiness, willingness, and

capacity.

**Readiness.** We are looking for a sober awareness of their inability to maintain a stable life and healthy relationships due to life-controlling issues (see list above) and a deep desire to overcome those issues or patterns and be restored to God's purpose for their life. In the beginning, in an interview setting for example, this is pretty challenging to evaluate. In other words, it is common for them to show signs of being ready initially but not end up being what many call "rock bottom." As long as we do not see a person as a violent threat or relationally toxic and divisive, often we will err on the side of giving them a chance.

**Willingness.** We are looking for evidence of a willingness to dramatically sacrifice personal freedoms, preferences, and comforts to experience long-term change. That evidence is exhibited by the self-awareness and humility it takes to receive instruction and restriction without becoming hardened and resentful toward the restorative process. It is not required or expected for participants to agree with or even understand all that is being asked of them, but if they have decided to fully and wholistically restore their lives, they will submit to the process out of trust that we have their best interest at heart.

**Capacity.** We are looking for men and women who can participate mentally, socially, physically, legally, and educationally in the program. Sadly, we have learned the hard lessons of trying to make a program like Restoration fit men and women who are not at a place in their life to engage or benefit from it as it has been built. There is a level of mental ability needed to participate educationally in environments where learning is taking place about sometimes difficult topics and material. There is a social and emotional ability needed to relate in healthy ways with program leaders as well as fellow participants, and there is a physical ability needed to participate in the regular schedule and activities of the program.

# Restored Lives

*You are the light of the world. A city set on a hill cannot be hidden. Nor do people light a lamp and put it under a basket, but on a stand, and it gives light to all in the house. In the same way, let your light shine before others, so that they may see your good works and give glory to your Father who is in heaven.*

**—Matthew 5:14–16**

The Restoration Program taught me what Paul describes in Galatians as the freedom in Christ that set me free! I no longer identify as an ex-drug addict, ex-prisoner, bad father, bad husband, or bad employee. I will never again give the enemy credit for anything or space in my life. I give all glory to the Creator of all things and know every outcome of every situation in my life is in His hands, and His will suits me well! I have left a life of drugs and destruction behind and am living a restored life.

**John Paul Davis (2019 Restoration Program Graduate)**

Thank you, Restoration, for the opportunity to become a new creation! Restoration meant restoring my relationship with the Father, Son, and Holy Spirit. By doing that, I am a free man who understands what commitment, responsibility, and self-control are. I have an ally in this world to guide me through. Blessed be God the Father and Lord Jesus Christ.

**Doug Sanders (2019 Restoration Program Graduate)**

The Restoration Program was such an invaluable and meaningful time in my life. After suffering with years of addiction and not knowing anything other than that lifestyle, I needed *all* that the program offered. Accountability, structure, and forming relationships with others on the same journey, desiring change, were instrumental. I'm forever grateful that the Lord used the restorative process at Victory Mission to help show me there is hope and true heart change in Jesus Christ.

**Matthew Hayes (2020 Restoration Program Graduate)**

Before the Restoration Program, I spent my life believing that I would never find happiness outside of a baggie and a pipe. After losing my children, during my third time in prison, before I heard the truth of the Gospel, it was at that point I decided to change my life, whatever it took. Through prayer I found myself at the mercy of a process I knew nothing about. The restorative process at Victory Mission took me on the journey of my life. I dedicated myself to it, and came face to face with myself and my problems. I was empowered through learning to submit to Spirit-led leaders, and to fully trust in every step and detail involved. I found myself growing at an accelerating velocity toward life transformation and a success I never would have dreamed possible before. Along the way, I attained a joy that came from an acquired belief in myself and a trust in the faithfulness and power of God. My life has been radically transformed. I'm completely unfamiliar with the person I used to be.

**Charles Romine (2020 Restoration Program Graduate)**

Before coming to the Restoration Program, I lived a life of violence and crime. Hopelessly addicted to whatever I could get my hands on, just to ease the pain. I had been tossed around the foster care system for the first six years of my life and struggled with finding a sense of belonging and identity throughout my entire life. I looked for these things in the street life, women, and various other things of this world. This led me to multiple prison sentences and abandoning the children I had along the way. During my last prison sentence, I had no place to go upon my release, and I had burned every bridge possible in my life.

That's where the Restoration Program at Victory Mission enters in my story. Upon arriving, I was welcomed and ushered into discipleship and a life of faith. I had no plans of changing, coming to the program, *but God* had different plans. I surrendered my life to the Lord and to the process laid out in Restoration, and God established me and did "immeasurably more" than I could have asked for at that time in my life.

Long story short, I now have my kids back in my life, am in full time ministry, own a house, and am married to a godly woman. But most importantly, I get to share the good news of the gospel of Jesus Christ every day of my life and watch from the front row as God changes and transforms what seems to be unchangeable. I will forever be indebted to the work that God has done through the Restoration Program.

**Noah Huskey (2020 Restoration Program Graduate)**

I once was hopeless. A man, but not really a man. My only concern was destruction. Violence, addiction, sexual impurity, and complete hatred were the only things I lived for. My isolation and addictions kept me captive for over fifteen years. This ultimately led me to prison, which was the best thing that ever happened to me. Because after prison, it led me to Victory Mission's Restoration Program.

That's where I met Jesus. That's where I also met good, godly men and women who changed the course of my life forever. The restorative process taught me how to be a man—something I thought I knew but I'd never come close to. Through the program, I now have full custody of my son and daughter, who I fought three years to get out of foster care. God gave me an amazing wife and blessed me with two beautiful stepdaughters. Restoration not only taught me how to live a life pleasing to God, but it also gave me back the things that I desired most, through my faith in and obedience to Him. It taught me to rethink everything about what the world says a man should be, and to be just who God made me to be. Restoration saved my life.

**Jacob Austin (2020 Restoration Program Graduate)**

When I came to the Restoration Program at Victory Mission, I was a mess, broken, lost, and full of anxiety. I was embraced with love, patience, and understanding from the staff and volunteers. I overcame my anxiety and depression through God's healing hand. After that, Victory Mission helped walk me through the steps and processes of gaining back a stable and fulfilling life and a relationship with Christ. I now manage the kitchen and garden for Victory Mission, I have my kids back in my life, and I walk in God's love and in my identity ... in Christ.

**Dyllan Dale (2020 Restoration Program Graduate)**

Victory Mission took me in at one of the lowest points in my life. With no one to turn to and nowhere to go, I was welcomed with love, and for the first time, I didn't have to act like someone I was not. Victory Mission gave me a safe place to learn who I was meant to be and to grow into the man God has called me to be. I learned what it meant to pursue a relationship with Christ, and soon I began to see restoration in all areas of my life. I am forever grateful and will always treasure what I learned during my time at Victory Mission.

**Cody Pickens (2020 Restoration Program Graduate)**

I came to Victory Mission's shelter after four years of homelessness. I was in the cycle of trying it my way, but after getting a job, car, or place and [then] ending up in jail and losing everything over and over again, I knew I needed something different. So I applied to the Restoration Program, was accepted the next day, and praised God. My expectations were to start going to church, to get a job, and with a year's sobriety, to move on with my life. God had other plans.

He was speaking to me and was telling me over and over that my children deserve to have a godly father, and I began implementing what that looks like. I was blessed by participating in Leadership Development Training while in Phases 1 and 2 of the program. I found my purpose as a leader, and Mark poured into us and taught us how to lead like Jesus. I took an internship with the Men's Shelter at the front desk, and God continued moving in my life. My children were coming to church with me and proud of their father as I held my head high, giving God all the glory. I am now a leader at my home church. I am an Outreach Chaplain Apprentice, overseeing the Emergency and Transitional Shelter at Victory Mission. I am so thankful to Mark McKnelly for putting together a program that works and for coming alongside and believing in us."

**Bobby Mitchell (2020 Restoration Program Graduate)**


When I got to the Restoration Program, I was met with nothing short of the love of Christ! They didn't see me as a broken-down, lost, hopeless addict; they saw me as a child of God and treated me as such! With the help of the Chaplain team and countless volunteers, I learned how to budget, how to build a resume, and countless other life skills. I got plugged into an awesome home church and, by the grace of God, was able to gain restoration with my family! My family and I are forever thankful for the Restoration Program at Victory Mission and the staff who give their time and talents to show a once-hopeless man like me how to live a life of victory!

**Michael Hayes (2021 Restoration Program Graduate)**

# About the Author

First and foremost, I am a child of God, a husband, a father of four, and now almost fourteen years in recovery from the addiction that nearly destroyed my life but also brought me to faith in Christ.

On January 24, 2008, I became a Christ-follower. Before then, I was a successful entrepreneur. In the final year I spent with the company I started and co-owned, it generated $5 million in annual revenue and employed over fifty people.

In 2009, I entered a full-time vocational ministry at Schweitzer Church in Springfield, Missouri. While on staff there, I planted an outreach service called Church @ the

Center and developed a one-year, in-depth discipleship program called the Life Change Plan for men and women in recovery housing. Both of these ministries were successful and instrumental in an important season of learning how to serve those in extreme poverty.

In 2017, I transitioned to the nonprofit world and became a chaplain at Victory Mission + Ministry in Springfield, Missouri. Since joining Victory Mission, I have developed the Restoration Program, for men and women reentering society from incarceration or recovering from addiction. As Director of Restoration, I now oversee a team of chaplains and chaplain apprentices who serve over three dozen participants while planning and preparing for the future expansion of the ministry.

I have over ten years of combined experience working in the trenches with those in extreme poverty, having served six years in benevolence ministry on staff at a church and now four years as a chaplain at a Christian nonprofit. My passion for the subject of long-term life change for those in material and relational poverty has only increased over my time in this ministry, even with a success rate most would struggle to see as successful.

# About Renown Publishing

Renown Publishing was founded with one mission in mind: to make your great idea famous.

At Renown Publishing, we don't just publish. We work hard to pair strategy with innovative marketing techniques so that your book launch is the start of something bigger.

Learn more at <u>RenownPublishing.com</u>.

# Notes

1. Lupton, Robert D. *Toxic Charity: How the Church Hurts Those They Help and How to Reverse It.* 1st edition. HarperOne, 2011.

2. Corbett, Steve, and Brian Fikkert. *When Helping Hurts: How to Alleviate Poverty Without Hurting the Poor ... and Yourself.* New edition. Moody Publishers, 2014.

3. *Merriam-Webster Dictionary,* "restoration". https://www.merriam-webster.com/dictionary/restoration.

4. *Official Report of the International Christian Endeavor Convention.* United Society of Christian Endeavor, 1896, p. 221.

5. Matthew 9:38. New American Standard Bible (NASB). The Lockman Foundation, 1995.

6. Matthew 9:38. Holy Bible, English Standard Version (ESV). Crossway, 2011.

7. Matthew 9:38. The Message. NavPress Publishing Group, 2002.

8.Chambers, Oswald. My Utmost for His Highest. Dodd, Mead & Co., 1935.

9. Vanderkam, Laura. *168 Hours: You Have More Time Than You Think*. Westminster, England: Portfolio, 2010.

10. Havner, Vance. *Jesus Only*. Shoals, Indiana: Kingsley Press, 2016.

11. Cloud, Henry, and John Townsend. *Boundaries*. Grand Rapids, Michigan: Zondervan, 2017.